Reiki Healing
and
Chakra Healing

2 BOOKS IN 1

Reiki Healing

Chakra Healing

Matthew Green

By reading this document, the reader agrees that under no circumstances is the author responsible for any losses, direct or indirect, which are incurred as a result of the use of information contained within this document, including, but not limited to, — errors, omissions, or inaccuracies.

4

List of Books

Reiki Healing

How to Improve Your Health and Increase Your Energy. A Step-by-Step Complete Guide to Self Healing Through Meditation to Achieve Physical and Spiritual Wellness

Matthew Green

Table of Contents

INTRODUCTION

There are plenty of books on this subject on the market, thanks again for choosing this one! Every effort was made to ensure it is full of as much useful information as possible, please enjoy!

WHAT IS REIKI?

It is the best way to use our inner energy. We all have it. Just not everyone knows how to direct it. The times we live in now are one of accelerated change, of anguish, not only individual, but also collective. We feel that time passes faster and science does not always give us the answers to these feelings.

There are new incurable diseases (AIDS, many types of cancer and bird flu, for example) and old diseases that are beginning to be difficult to treat (such as tuberculosis). Countries are disintegrating socially, because the fury of nature (which often leads to epidemics, as well as all material destruction) and people are homeless, experiencing serious difficulties.

Our Planet is undergoing sudden changes in its interior and atmosphere, with hurricanes, earthquakes, fires, erupting volcanoes, prolonged droughts and floods (often out of season). Studies point out that there is no more water to support the planet's population for years to come, where our grandchildren and great-grandchildren will have to fetch it in situations other than ours. Soil and atmosphere are contaminated by pollutants of all kinds such as CFC's, sulfur compounds and so on.

All kinds of violence are glaring facts in today's life. Children, once considered easy prey, are becoming great predators. Just see what happens in many slums and with some fanatical sects.

We are in a time of transformation, where a new life begins. The life that is born now is fragile and its survival is still uncertain due to the evils we have done to our planet and the drastic changes in our customs driven by appearances created by a collective mind that does nothing for those most in need .

We can all clearly see and feel this birth. There is an awareness of the need to purify the earth and our attitude toward it. A new consciousness is being born slowly.

This is clearly represented by the women's voices saying "no" to abuse, violence, screaming "yes" to peaceful change and compassion. It is the return to the old form of perception and feeling, values that are missing in modern life. We need to realize who we really are: sentient beings, healers. Conscious participants of life!
We have noticed the return of healing methods such as the use of herbs, homeopathies, massages, flower essences, acupuncture, and others. Reiki is one such method and we consider it the greatest potential for kindness that can be given to the people of this planet. It is available to anyone and children can use it too. It is a neutral method with no negative consequences. It belongs to everyone and to the earth itself.

This is the time to heal the earth, people and animals. There is no way to postpone. A new day will be of pain, suffering and crisis for the world. We must recognize the need for healing for all people in these times of pain and planetary change.

If what led you to read this book is just wanting to know more, I hope to contribute to your knowledge.

But if what led you to read this book was also your inner Master's call to become a Reikian Healer, I advise you to put your Energy into it through writing so that it becomes your Magic Diary.

The ritual we will propose now is simple and easy to perform. It will serve to bless this now becoming your Magic Diary. Performing it is not indispensable. But if you do, you will feel the Sacred Energy flowing. The path of spirituality calls for firm postures and discipline. The act of consecrating your Diary is a custom that comes from ancient healers.

You only need a candle, a packet of dried herbs or incense (the herbs or incense that are commonly used are fennel, sage or lavender) and a pen.

On a full moon night, place the book, candle, pen, and incense on a table. Light the candle and recite the following evocation for the book:

"By strength, will and potent power,
The spirits I invoke in this hour of ritual,
To endow this book with wisdom,
To launch the perfect rite and enchantment"
Open the book and on the first page draw a Pentagram with the pen. In the center of the Pentagram write your name or the name you use as "nick name", which is your magic name. Close the

book and light the incense. When it begins to burn, pass the book through the cleansing smoke saying:

"All negative thoughts are banished,
All unwanted vibrations disappear,
Only the forces and powers of the good that I desire will be here from that moment. "
Blow out the candle and the herbs. Store your book in a safe place. You will put your ideas, which are your energies, into it, so it is advisable that other people do not handle your book.
May Unconditional Love vibrate in all hearts!

CHAPTER 1
THE HISTORY OF REIKI

The traces of Reiki go far back in human history. In every culture of the world, there were people who had access to higher states of consciousness, and thus timeless wisdom, which they transmitted to humankind and were then passed on, usually orally, by priests, saints, and teachers. There are many indications that in all advanced civilizations - among the Mayans as well as the Egyptians and the ancient Greeks - it was known how to directly tap light energy. In any case, the cosmic symbols on which the Reiki system is based can be found in the Mayan pyramids as well as in the Temple of Luxor.

The historian and Reiki teacher Dr. Barbara Ray traced the roots of Reiki to about 6000 years before Christ and found that they are in northern India and Tibet. The cosmic symbols on which the Reiki system is based are as well known to the Tibetan Lamas as the associated attunement processes.

Dr. Although Mikao Usui (1865-1926) is regarded as the founder of Reiki, but he has not invented this method, but merely rediscovered her and given her the name Reiki. Usui was one of the people who, like many people today, yearned for truth and enlightenment. According to tradition, he lived as the head of a Christian seminary in Kyoto, Japan, where he was repeatedly asked by his disciples about the phenomenon of the healings that

Jesus Christ had accomplished. He knew that Jesus had healed people by laying on hands - that's what the Bible says - but he wondered how that worked. He even traveled to the United States and earned a doctorate in theology from the University of Chicago, but he wasn't any closer to the mystery of the early Christian healings.

Disappointed Usui returned to Japan, learned Sanskrit and began to occupy himself in a monastery with ancient Buddhist scriptures. Finally, he found the key to very ancient knowledge: a Sanskrit formula based on a set of cosmic or universal symbols. Whenever these symbols are activated, they activate the connection to the universal life force. The psychologist Carl Gustav Jung, who has studied cosmic symbols intensively, calls these symbols "foundations of humanity" and "the deepest knowledge available to humanity."

Based on these cosmic symbols is the attunement ritual of Reiki teachers. It goes back to instructions that Usui, according to legend, received in the following ways: He fasted and meditated for 21 days on a sacred mountain near Kyoto. On the last day, he had a light show shortly before sunrise. In front of a wall of light the Sanskrit formula with which he had worked so intensely appeared in golden letters. He took the cosmic symbols on which the entire Reiki system is based, in a certain order true, together with the corresponding attunement processes. All this burned deep into his memory. This experience could be called an experience of enlightenment or cosmic initiation.

According to legend, Usui injured on the way back to the village on a stone. His toe was bleeding, but when he held his hands over it, the bleeding stopped immediately. Arriving in the valley, he ordered a big Japanese breakfast in an inn. It tasted great, and he tolerated it, even though he had fasted for three weeks. The daughter of the host, who suffered from toothache for days, he laid his hands on briefly - and she was freed from her complaints. These first "healing miracles" exemplify how Reiki can be used: as emergency aid at the scene of an accident, to harmonize bodily functions and in case of both acute and chronic physical and emotional complaints.

Dr. Usui called his method Reiki. Rei means "universal" and ki means "life force". Reiki means "method for activating universal life force". Initially, Dr. Usui also had many beggars in the slums of Kioto and joined them in Reiki. However, he soon realized that they did not practice it. They preferred the poor but comfortable life of a beggar and did not want to take responsibility for their own lives.

It is also said that Dr. Usui lit a torch in broad daylight in Kyoto and walked up and down the promenade. Asked what he wanted with the torch in bright sunshine, he replied that he was looking for people who wanted to see the true light. This began his lecture and seminar time. At the end of his life, he had taught many people in Reiki and shared his inner knowledge with several advanced disciples. One of these students was Dr. Chujiro Hayashi, who led a private Reiki clinic in Tokyo until 1940.

The five rules of life of Dr. Usui:

- Do not be angry.
- Do not worry.
- Be thankful.
- Do your duty.
- Be friendly to your fellow human beings.

Hawayo Takata, an American-born American, traveled to Tokyo in 1933 because she was suffering from a serious illness and wanted to die with her family, but things turned out differently. After being dr. Chujiro Hayashi's clinic was treated with Reiki, she was five months later cured and now wanted to become a Reiki teacher. Dr. Hayashi not only agreed but even made Hawayo Takata his successor and gave her all the knowledge of Reiki to save it from the turmoil of World War II. So the Reiki knowledge found its way to the west, to Hawaii, where Hawayo Takata returned in 1937.

However, the first Reiki seminar on the American mainland took place only at the end of the 1970s. This was also Dr. Barbara Ray. The scientist, who focused on ancient cultures, intuitively recognized at her first intuition that she had found something she had been searching for the last time in vain: the knowledge of how universal energy can be directly tapped and activated.

Hawayo Takata trained 22 Reiki teachers in the US and Canada before she died in December 1980 at the age of 80. A year before she died, she had been with Dr. Barbara Ray founded the American Reiki Association (AIRA) and Ray at the inaugural event of her Successor appointed. Many assume that Ms. Takata also joins her granddaughter Phyllis Furomoto in Reiki, but only in three grades, not the seven-step system that corresponds to our chakras or main energy centers. Phyllis Furomoto founded thein 1982 in Hawaii Reiki Alliance. In a personal conversation with me, Ms. Furomoto admitted that she knew only three degrees but did not want to deny that there was more.

At this point, I do not want to go into this discussion any further. The only important thing is that Reiki "works" and that it is the original system that only activates universal energy.

CHAPTER 2
WHAT IS REIKI AND HOW DOES IT WORK?

The word Reiki consists of the syllables Rei for "universal" and ki for "life force" and, as already stated, denotes a system for activating the universal life force. You may know the Japanese word ki because it is also part of aikido, the name of a far-eastern martial art. It corresponds to the Chinese word chi (recently also often qi written), which is also found in chi gong or tai chi, the name of techniques that also have the goal of increasing the vitality.

Albert Einstein has found that mass is equal to energy and that even a dormant body - however firm and solid it may seem to us - must contain energy because it has mass. How big this energy is can be calculated by means of its famous formula $E = mc^2$. The c in this formula is the way for the speed of light, measured in meters per second. In the conversion of mass into energy, so also the speed plays a role or the frequency with which the individual particles vibrate, from the mass or matter ultimately exists.

In terms of our body - or rather, our body system - this means that the particles that make up our physical body swing the slowest. At this level, Reiki can eliminate energy blockages and cure illnesses.

Slightly faster, the particles vibrate on the next level, the level of our emotions. Here, Reiki can make us no longer easily identify with external events and find cheerful serenity and inner peace. This happens mainly because the thoughts slow down. And that brings us into contact with higher levels of consciousness, such as the level of our intuition. The better our connection to the intuitive level, the more our life comes to flow and as a result, we automatically do the right thing at the right time and let it be wrong.

At the Temple of the Oracle at Delphi, it said, "Man, know yourself." If we were just bodies, feelings, and thoughts, that might be relatively easy, but there is much more to discover.

On the level of intuition, there are other, ever-higher levels of consciousness, and finally the level with the highest vibration frequency - the highest energy level in the universe. This very high vibration, with which we all came into the world, is known in different cultures under different names. The Russians call them "bioplasma," the Kahunas in Hawaii speak of "mana," in India they call them "pranas," and for Christians, this energy is simply called "light." "You are light," says Christ to his disciples, or, "You are the light of the world."

I find "light" as the name for the highest energy in the universe very suitable because light has the property to emit in all directions. This very high vibration, this light energy or cosmic energy makes up our so-called "radiation". This light shines through our eyes, because as William Shakespeare said, "The eyes are the windows of the soul."

And this is where authentic Reiki comes into play. During the four first-degree attunements, our ability to emit light energy is permanently increased - at least doubled. Our charisma will be significantly improved, and that will have consequences: people with a better charisma will magically attract positive people and events. It is just as the proverbs say: "As you call into the forest, it sounds out." Or: "Equal and like to join." That our charisma has improved permanently, we can also see how pets or smaller children respond to us.

Another consequence of the attunements is that the light energy or universal energy is concentrated, especially in the hands. Every time we place our hands in the future, be it ourselves, other humans, animals or plants, only universal light energy is activated. As a result of the four attunements, our seven major energy centers (chakras) are developing in a harmonious way, and we become more permeable to the highest vibration in the universe. When we lay hands on ourselves or others in the future, the light energy automatically flows to where it is most needed or where the cause of disharmony lies. This then leads us to recognize why we have created a particular disease. It has served its purpose and we do not need it anymore. In this sense, Reiki is above all a self-help technique that always looks holistic and causal. The energy flows where it is needed most to bring us into contact with its real causes through a cognition, and in addition, to that clarity also gives us the power to eliminate the causes or change our attitude - if we want to.

For example, if you have a runny nose and you treat yourself to Reiki in the beginning, you, with the help of your Higher Self, that omniscient entity in us all, see why he is "snuffed" or "fed up" with it. Has he recognized that the cold usually disappears very quickly.

Authentic Reiki always puts us in touch with our true needs. When we are exhausted, it gives us more energy, when we are nervous, it brings peace and serenity. If we are tired and ecstatic at night, we can fall asleep more easily with Reiki. The same thing happens when we treat another human being: the universal energy also puts him in touch with his real needs.

We can apply Reiki anytime, anywhere: watching TV (the news becomes easier to digest), talking on the phone, on the bus, at the grocery store, as a sleep aid and as a means of test anxiety. For someone who is once properly attuned, Reiki functions as automatically as breathing - without thought, belief or concentration.

With Reiki, we can also make foods more digestible and energize water. In authentic Reiki, we work exclusively with universal energy, the strongest vibration in the universe. This energy is always supportive, has no side effects and can not be overdosed. The more we activate, the more it flows because we are connected to an inexhaustible source of universal energy.

The amazing thing about Reiki is the boost of consciousness that most people experience almost immediately. I consider Reiki a path to enlightenment with healing as a welcome accompaniment. Radiant health is our natural birthright or as the famous philosopher Arthur Schopenhauer puts it: "Health is not everything. But without health everything is nothing" We cannot miss anything we do not know. Radiant health is not the absence of disease but a condition in the morning - every morning! - want to embrace the world, full of zest for life and enthusiasm.

Reiki helps us in our holistic growth process and helps us recognize our human weaknesses, accept them and let them go, to become more complete. Maybe Reiki is "only" a way to perfection?

CHAPTER 3 - WHAT'S SO GOOD ABOUT REIKI?

Reiki is the art and method to activate and apply natural, universal life energy for harmony, healing, and holistic development. Reiki always has a holistic and causal effect.

Reiki is easy to learn by everyone, including children.

Reiki promotes healing and wholeness, prevents disorders and maintains true well-being at any age.

Reiki is a self-help technique that you can use for others to relieve stress and experience deep relaxation.

Reiki creates a balance of life energy in an amount that promotes your health and well-being at all levels.

Reiki vitalizes your entire organism.

Reiki balances you on all levels: the physical, the emotional, the mental and the spiritual.

Reiki is a natural healing method that can be combined with all other healing methods, whether alternatively holistic or traditional medicine.

Reiki is not a belief system or a worldview. You do not need to believe it for it to work.

Reiki can also be used successfully in animals and plants.

Reiki is completely safe to use.

Reiki brings you in touch with your inner qualities: joy in being, compassion, unconditional love, divine peace and serenity, and promotes harmonious growth.

Reiki helps you to transform and attain enlightenment.

Reiki, so to speak, is a path to enlightenment, and healing at all levels is a welcome accompaniment.

CHAPTER 4

FEATURES OF UNIVERSAL ENERGY

Understanding what properties have universal energy means understanding how Reiki works and what it brings us. I've put together some features that must be met so you can be sure that this is the original, authentic Reiki. If only one of the features is not met, it is not the original energy system. So it is not enough that a Reiki teacher is sympathetic. In a modification of a previously quite well-known advertising slogan, one could say: "I only leave universal energy on my chakras!" That means: I do not want my therapist to work with personal energy, because I do not want to absorb any negative vibrations. Only the best should be good enough for us. After all, we are children of God!

1.   Universal energy and the authentic Reiki to activate this energy always work for the benefit of the recipient, never negative. Universal energy always puts the recipient in touch with their real needs. Even when healing crises emerge, in authentic Reiki, we work directly with our "higher self" or the agency of wisdom within us who knows exactly what and how much they can "feel" us, and what and how much we » can "digest" - on the physical, the mental or the spiritual level. Healing crises are rare, but when such a crisis occurs, it means: not less, but give more Reiki! Authentic Reiki does not "invent" anything, but only brings to the surface what is there so that it can be processed as soon

as possible. If we have learned the lesson associated with a particular disease, we do not need it anymore!

2.   If, like authentic Reiki, we work exclusively with universal energy, there are no limitations in the application. Universal energy is always harmless to use, there is no "too much" and no negative side effects. If you read in Reiki books or hear from Reiki teachers that the elderly, the sick, or children are only allowed to be treated for a short time, be skeptical. Universal energy is always harmless, so the longer, the better!

3.   When working exclusively with universal energy, the practitioner can not feel exhausted or drained by the application. Universal energy is over personal. Through the attunements and treatments, we join in an inexhaustible source of this energy. The more treatments we give, the better we feel: more relaxed, activated, clearer, depending on what we need right now. The best we can do as a Reiki practitioner is several treatments in a row. My record is seven treatments in one day and 27 in a week. After that, I felt like after a deep meditation - which Reiki is also.

4.   When we work exclusively with universal energy, we can not absorb any negative vibrations in the application. Universal energy is the subtlest and strongest energy in the universe at the same time. As you may know from physics, more subtle energies are stronger than coarser ones, higher ones superimpose low ones. Thus, we are protected when treating before recording negative vibrations. When, once we have been properly attuned

by a competent teacher, we bring our hands close to a living being, we transform everything negative and neutralize it.

5.   When we work exclusively with Universal Energy, regardless of how the person feels, whether he is awake or asleep, whether or not he or she believes in Reiki, that energy works. Universal energy is the most powerful in the entire universe and therefore able to penetrate and transform the energy of all outer planes. Also, just as we are "on top" on the outer levels, it does not matter for the success of the treatment. During the treatment, the therapist and the treated person harmonize equally. When we breathe, we do not need to think about how well the oxygen is doing us. This does not make breathing more effective. The same applies to a Reiki treatment.

6.   Universal energy is always holistic and causal. Authentic Reiki is a holistic causal therapy or causal whole-body therapy. Universal energy flows by itself to where it is most needed, where the causes of disharmony lie - no matter on what level. So it's not about symptom management, even if symptoms can disappear. The duration of the healing process varies and depends not so much on the nature or duration of the disease, but on the willingness of the individual to learn from his illness or not.

7.   Before or after an authentic Reiki treatment, neither cleansing nor harmonization exercises are necessary. Once properly tuned, we can do nothing but activate universal energy. Therefore, we do not need to ask for Reiki power before the

treatment and not for the assistance of angels. Universal energy releases blockages on all levels and harmonizes the aura, our subtle energy field. Since we can not absorb any negative vibrations during the treatment, we do not need to keep our hands under cold water afterwards.

8.   With universal energy, we can not manipulate or pursue selfish ends. We bring the one to whom we send this energy exclusively in contact with his real needs. Universal energy is always harmless and supportive. In that sense, we do not need to ask anyone if we are allowed to handle him remotely. If we kindly think of someone or pray for someone, we do not ask for permission before. We can ask little children, babies, animals, and plants, but we will not get a clear answer from them. So should they all go away empty? That would be a shame.

9. When we work exclusively with Universal Energy, that energy always works in harmony with the Higher Self on all levels. Universal energy "knows" where the causes of a problem lie and automatically flows there to make them aware and dissolve. We are dealing with the best therapist in the world, our Higher Self. It helps us learn and grow 24 hours a day. When we listen inward during the Reiki treatment, we get an answer to our question about the cause of the event - in the form of a sentence, a feeling, a dream or a picture.

10. Authentic Reiki, in which we work exclusively with universal energy, harmonizes with all forms of therapy, with all methods of personal growth, with all worldviews, religions and meditation

techniques. With Reiki we activate the most natural energy of the world with which we have already been born. The authentic Reiki is not inconsistent with any treatment, be it homeopathic or orthodox medical treatments. Reiki promotes and accelerates the healing process. It alleviates the negative side effects of medication or radiation and reinforces the positive ones. People who take tablets should hold them in their hands for a while before swallowing to increase their vibration.

Authentic Reiki puts us in touch with our divine essence, which mystics speak for millennia. If we believe in God, it deepens that belief, but atheists also benefit from it. Anything we've already benefited from, like yoga, tai chi, or meditation, should be kept as Reiki comes along because Reiki enhances the positive effects of all other mind-expanding methods.

Even if only one of these ten characteristics is not true, it can not be the original Reiki method, because it only activates universal energy.

CHAPTER 5
REIKI AND THE CHAKRAS

Reiki is chakra work. That is, we work on the seven main energy centers that lie along the spine in the subtle body. Via the crown or crown chakra, we absorb light energy. This energy then flows from top to bottom through one center after another and is transformed in each chakra so that it can be used for our physical level - organs, glands. Finally, at the root center, it unites with the earth energy that we constantly absorb through the soles of our feet.

Chakras are not static points, but moving light wheels - as their name implies (the Sanskrit word chakra means "wheel"). They are dynamic or rotating centers that distribute light energy in all directions, like small suns. The movement is created by the life energy that flows into the respective chakra and brings it to life. When the life force is in flux, the chakras begin to vibrate and bloom. The more life force flows through them, the more beautiful they bloom, and this is visible in our charisma.

"Thou shalt acquire riches in the heavens, not on earth," says the Bible. We do this by working with Reiki and other types of meditation on our charisma. What we achieve in this way remains with us. If it were part of the physical body, it would be lost with death and we would have to start all over again, but this progress is not part of the physical body but is stored in the etheric body.

With the authentic Reiki, we bring about a harmonious development of our energy centers. The chakras, which are not as advanced as others, evolve over time and flourish. You can really visualize this as the blossoming of a flower bud in the sunlight: we are becoming more and more permeable to the light energy and the flow of life energy within us is getting stronger. It all happens in a gentle way. The universal energy activated in the attunements is always harmless and supportive and always depends on the real needs of the recipient. Overstraining or "too much" is thus excluded.

All degrees of authentic Reiki develop all seven chakras, but the emphasis is always on the energy center associated with the corresponding degree. In the first degree, especially the root or base center is activated. We lose our existential fears and get a positive relationship to responsibility and matter. The second degree emphasizes the sacral chakra, the seat of sensuality, sexuality, creativity, and reproduction. Little by little, we recognize our divine potential and live it. In the third degree, above all, the solar network is activated, the seat of our self-confidence and our self-esteem. The fourth degree has a special relation to the heart chakra, the chakra of love. By developing this center, we develop our humanity and can feel, love, cry, laugh, share, empathize and pray. We become love. Doubt and suspicion disappear as well as hairiness and too much disinterestedness. Instead, trust floods the heart. In deep meditation or in Reiki you are connected to the whole of creation, from heart to heart, beyond mind and language.

In the fifth degree, especially the connection between heart and neck is strengthened. Our love becomes more meditative. We feel the desire to share love with each other. With the sixth degree, which especially activates the third eye, our consciousness is increasingly developing in the direction of: "I am love." When the energy in the sixth chakra is awakened, it is experienced as a tremendous expansion, as a possibility, a glimpse to throw cosmic or infinite.

When the energy flows freely in the seventh or crown chakra, we finally arrive home. A waking crown chakra corresponds to the seventh day of creation on which the Creator rests. There is nothing left to do. Only now that we have become masters of ourselves can we really help others. It is also called "Unio Mystica," the mystical union of yin and yang. Only at this highest summit of synthesis is true, lasting fulfillment possible.

However, it's less about knowing about the chakras than about feeling them authentic. Working on the chakras - and this is Reiki - serves to dissolve energy blockages. When in the end all seven chakras have become so active that they merge into a single pillar of light, it is called enlightenment.

CHAPTER 6

TREAT YOURSELF AND OTHERS WITH REIKI

The first degree is the most important in the seven-level system of authentic Reiki, in which the participants come into contact with the Universal Energy, the most gentle, subtle yet powerful energy in the universe once and for all. Even if someone had not done Reiki for 20 years, the contact with this ultimate vibration would still be there. The effect lasts a lifetime and even beyond. Whenever we bring our hands close to a living being after reaching the first degree - close to ourselves, other humans, animals or plants - universal energy is activated. Universal energy is always harmless and supportive. We can not manipulate that energy. There is also no "too much" of it, so no overdose and no side effects. However, it sometimes happens that old symptoms flare up again during the causal and holistic healing process. Then one speaks of an "initial aggravation" or "reaction," as we can observe them in other holistic therapies such as Bach flowers or classical homeopathy. To shorten the healing process, it means: give more Reiki, not less.

But Reiki does much more than cure disease. On the way to our true nature, the physical, mental and emotional levels harmonize as well. With the first degree, we may experience that we no longer or only rarely become ill. When the energy in our system flows freely, and it does so through regular Reiki treatments, eventually all blockages will be resolved and no new ones will emerge, but only energy blockages can lead to physical and emotional problems. With the first degree, we, therefore, have a holistic and causal health system in our hands. We practice by making sure we do not get sick at all. A better health care reform that really deserves this name can not exist in my eyes.

With Reiki, we keep our energies flowing at all levels, and more and more come into contact with our real needs, including in terms of nutrition, relaxation, and exercise. The first degree strengthens our immune system and activates our self-healing powers. Often participants come to the 1st-degree seminar because they themselves have a physical or mental problem or because someone from their relatives or friends has such a problem and they want to help him. Reiki gives us the inner clarity needed to recognize the causes of an event, and the power to change our mindset so that a mental or physical illness becomes superfluous. We learn the lesson that was associated with the problem, and with it, symptoms can disappear overnight.

In the first degree, there is a harmonious development of all our energy centers, with particular emphasis on the root or base center. In this center we are rooted, here we feel grounded. When the energy in this chakra flows freely, we lose our fears of the future and our existence, better understand the material plane, take on more willing responsibility, and trust ourselves much more. The freer the energy flows in the root center, the less we judge and condemn ourselves and others and the more positive and constructive our attitude becomes to life, to ourselves and to others.

"Is the glass half full or half empty?" If we are to judge, we are increasingly choosing to see the positives in each situation and be content with what we have and are. Our relationships become more authentic, loving and honest. Many make "clear ship" in their relationships and forgive, for example, their parents or finally have the courage to clarify overdue with their boss. The first degree also enables us to deal better with stressful situations. We can now respond to situations that would have overwhelmed us with serenity and humor.

However, with the first degree, we also open up to our intuitive level. We notice, for example, that we are increasingly doing the right thing from the inside out and let it be wrong. On the spiritual level, we realize that we do not need to look for happiness in the outer world, because we can find something much more precious and enduring in us, namely divine peace. At first only occasionally, but then more and more clearly and constantly we learn that we are divine in our essence and that God does not dwell "in heaven" but in us. We realize that God has not forgotten us. We forgot him! And since God is part of us, we can never turn away from Him.

Energetic construction of ourselves (scheme)

Every day we should give ourselves a full Reiki treatment. With every position, we cover at least one chakra as well as many glands and internal organs. So we can benefit from universal energy at all levels. As we open our hearts, we become more alive and radiate unconditional love. The Bible says, "Love your neighbor as yourself." and "Become like children." Now we know an effective way to develop our capacity for love from the heart chakra and to get in touch with our "inner child," the Source of joy of life, enthusiasm, and enthusiasm. The first step is the beginning of a journey into the unknown, to our true, divine nature.

CHAPTER 7
REIKI WITHOUT ATTUNEMENTS

At the heart of a rehearsal course are the so-called "attunements." In the first degree, you get four attunements, in the second, one, in each further degree, one, and in the seventh degree, three. In addition, from Grade IIIA, so-called "reinforcing" attunements, which permanently extend our capacity for the respective grades, are added. In these attunements, the trained and competent Reiki teacher uses certain universal, cosmic symbols in a specific, traditional order to expand the channel that connects the chakras from within and the chakra assigned to each degree is to activate especially intense. Therefore you can not teach yourself Reiki. You need a competent teacher who gives you the votes.

If you want to get to know the effect of Reiki before you decide to participate in a Reiki seminar, you can work with a trick. Authentic Reiki uses only universal energy. This energy, in its essence, is the power of unconditional love. Our heart center is constantly radiating, whether we are aware of it or not, that highest vibration in the universe. Our arms and hands are as an extension of the heart chakra, to spread unconditional love. If we stay in the heart center during treatment with our consciousness now, we will work exclusively with this power - just like after a Reiki initiation.

So while we treat ourselves or others, we focus on our heart chakra in the middle of the chest and give the impulse to our heart: "Give!" The heart center can not do anything else than unconditional love. Like a small sun, it radiates this vibration uninterruptedly. When thoughts get in the way and we notice, we immediately return to our hearts with our attention and say, "Give!".

This is a beautiful heart meditation, in which we activate a lot of healing energy. Only through the power of unconditional love is healing possible. If we do not have a degree of Reiki, then we will not activate so much of this healing power, but enough to gain initial and profound experience with this energy. Once we 'get the taste', we may want to earn at least the first degree of Reiki, and that would indeed have some advantages. Once we are properly and competently attuned, it does not matter what we think. If we then bring our hands close to a living thing, we activate only universal energy, whether we are aware of it or not. This harmonizes body, soul, and spirit, and over time, blockages on all levels dissolve, allowing this energy to flow through us more and more freely and our charisma becomes ever stronger.

This is the sensational part of a course in achieving the first level of Reiki: We will be attached to the power of unconditional love for all eternity and from now on we will have a much greater capacity than without attunement. With first and second level attunements, our ability to work with light energy is at least doubled. By reaching the third degree, she has even quadrupled!

So you can do it without attunements, but with them, you can really relax during the Reiki treatments and you do not have to concentrate on something specific or think about something specific.

CHAPTER 8

RECOMMENDATIONS FOR THE REIKI
TREATMENT

Make sure you are not disturbed.

Calm, relaxing music can be helpful.

Wash your hands before the treatment.

Please remove the person to be treated, glasses and shoes.

Make it comfortable for you and the person to be treated, so that the outer ones do not distract from the inner experiences. The ideal is a padded Reiki couch at the right height with plenty of legroom for the practitioner, a sturdy dining table or a mat on the floor. Place a pillow under the head and under the knees of the person to be treated, if he wishes, and cover him with a blanket. Always give full treatment, except in case of accidents, emergencies and acute stress.

Hold each position for about five minutes. If you can not or do not want to touch the person directly, you can also hold your hands a few inches above their respective positions.

Arms and legs should not be crossed so as not to interfere with blood circulation.

If you know why the person wants to have a Reiki treatment, you can choose a suitable additional position.

If you are giving Reiki to someone for the first time and you have serious problems, it would be good to treat it on three consecutive days, for example on Friday, Saturday and Sunday. This provides so much energy that it quickly overcomes any possible healing crises. Reiki does not "invent" anything, but only brings to the surface what is there, so that it can be processed.

A little Reiki is basically better than no Reiki. If you have less time, just make fewer positions.

You can continue the treatments indefinitely, but at least until harmony and health is restored.

CHAPTER 9

THE TWELVE POSITIONS AND THEIR EFFECTS ON BODY, SOUL, AND SPIRIT

The Twelve-Position treatment is the technique for activating Universal Energy that you learn in the first degree and hopefully will accompany you through all the degrees you will ever learn. Above all, we work with these positions on our main energy centers or chakras. As they spin, these energy centers distribute universal or light energy throughout the body and into the extremities. With full treatment, we cover all possible causes of disharmony.

Through the four attunements of the first degree, we are tuned once and for all to the universal energy. That is, we have the guarantee to activate only universal energy. Only universal energy is always supportive, can not be overdosed, has no side effects, and puts ourselves and the people we treat in contact with our or their true needs.

Reiki always seems causal and holistic. That is, we never work only on the physical level. In the following pages, I describe the effects of the twelve positions of full treatment on the physical, emotional, mental and spiritual levels. You do not need to believe in these effects. If you practice Reiki, you will experience it yourself. However, every person is unique. It may well be that you make experiences that are not described here. Then rather trust your own experience than this book!

Reiki treatments are holistic, in the sense that the twelve items of full treatment affect each level at all levels. So it does not matter if the migraine we are suffering from is mainly mental or mostly physical.

Universal energy always finds its way to the causes of an event and, in addition to the knowledge about it, also gives us the power to change our attitude to it. Thus, healing becomes possible in the sense of becoming whole. Of course, you can also benefit from Reiki if you have no physical or mental problems. Use the energy for your spiritual development, experience states of consciousness such as joy in being, unity consciousness, divine peace and swimming in the sea of unconditional love. As the highest and therefore most powerful vibration in the Universe, Universal Energy is able to transform all lower vibrations - body, thoughts, feelings - and to advance our spiritual development.

The First Head Position

Physical level: At the first head position, we cover the pituitary gland and the Pineal gland off. The pituitary gland is our "master gland," because it controls all other glands. The glands act on the hormone secretion on all physical processes and also on our feelings. The pineal gland absorbs light energy and transforms it so that it is available to our body. It produces the hormone melatonin, which not only provides deep and healthy sleep but is also one of the most potent antioxidants we know. As you age, melatonin production decreases. With the first head position, we activate and harmonize the function of these two glands. At the same time, we cover our eyes. Anyone who has eye problems, such as short or long-sightedness, or often suffers from tired eyes, can feel an improvement over time. When we do Reiki, the effect is always towards balance and harmony. Over time, many people perceive colors brighter, more brilliant. We also cover the sinuses with this position. So if you have chronic sinusitis or runny nose, you will benefit from this position. In case of a cold, it helps to ask, "Why am I snuffling?" or, "What, perhaps by whom, are you fed up?" By doing so, we work together with our Higher Self, the instance of Wisdom and omniscience, and can significantly shorten the healing process. In addition, with this position, we cover teeth and jaws and do something to strengthen enamel and gums.

On the emotional level too, we benefit from the first position in the head. It helps us when we have fears, suffer from stress, trouble or worry. Over time, we see things more relaxed and can find our way back to our midst, releasing fears and worries. We shield ourselves against too many impressions from the outside.

On the mental or mental level, we benefit from this position because it makes our thoughts calmer, clearer, more positive, and more constructive. When we feel overwhelmed and apply this position, we are better able to prioritize, focus, gather inwardly, and find so-called "third-way solutions." These are solutions that benefit everyone involved, not one party at the expense of the other. The fact that this position calms the thoughts, we can regenerate with their help in a surprisingly short time. In the evening, it helps us to draw a curtain before our consciousness, let go of thoughts and fall asleep more easily, or fall asleep faster if we wake up in the middle of the night. Almost all sleep problems are solved with the first degree, usually during the seminar.

At the spiritual level, the first head position causes us to come into more contact with our inner guidance. In addition, by activating our crown center, we become more receptive to higher energies and, even in everyday situations, remain easier in a meditative state or in our midst. We no longer identify easily with our problems or the problems of others and remain cheerful and relaxed even in stressful situations.

With the first head position, we are developing more and more Unity or Cosmic Consciousness. We realize that the good of the whole includes ours too. Our desire is to look beyond the borders of our individual interests and to serve this whole more and more. This will make us happy and happy and never feel alone again.

The Second Head Position Or Temples Position

Together with the third, the second head position or temporal position on the physical level causes an improvement in headache and migraine. Like all Reiki positions we can also use these prophylactic, so it does not even come to complaints. Again, the plexus and pituitary glands are brought into balance. This position also helps with motion sickness.

On the emotional level, we benefit from this position because it stimulates the release of endorphins, so-called feel-good or

56

happiness hormones, that the body produces to maintain or restore a state of emotional wellbeing. So we can use this position to profit from depression, worry, stress, anxiety and other mental health problems. If we feel acutely depressed, we should immediately apply this position so that this condition does not solidify, but of course, the position also acts preventively. We experience more cheerful serenity and can better remember our dreams. This position balances the left and right halves of the brain and promotes the connection between the two hemispheres. The right brain represents intuition, holistic thinking, emotions, and creativity; the left stands for rational thinking, analytical thinking, and intellect. In many people, the connection between the two halves of the brain, the so-called "beam" is not particularly well developed. There are too few nerve connections or synapses, which causes the halves of the brain to work uncoordinated and sometimes even against each other. This Reiki position promotes harmonization of the two halves of the brain, ensuring that they work better together in the future. The first three head positions also activate more gray cells in the brain. In the average person, at most one-third of all nerve cells in the brain is active, while the largest part, so to speak, is in deep sleep.

On the mental level, the position causes our thoughts to become calmer, clearer, more positive, and more constructive, and our attitudes to many topics change. We see more and more challenges as challenges and experience crises as times of growth. Our creativity is stimulated and we become more productive, that is, we realize more of our ideas. Both our long-term memory and our short-term memory can improve over time.

At the spiritual level or level of personality development, we activate the crown center and the third eye. This means that we become more permeable to light energy, recognize our tasks in life more clearly and refine our perception. We become more open and our views become more universal.

The Third Head Position

In the third head position, we cover two important brain centers on the physical level: the speech center and the weight center. Those who have problems to express themselves clearly and may suffer from stuttering will benefit greatly from this position. In the weight center, our individual ideal weight is stored, similar to the desired room temperature in a thermostat. This individual ideal weight may differ greatly from the healthy ideal weight, both up and down. If we hold this position for a longer time, the values will become more and more equal, and we will effortlessly reach the optimal ideal weight for us. As already mentioned, this position also prevents headaches and migraine attacks and helps in the acute case. The position also has a favorable effect on the eyes and thus on the eyesight. It makes you easier in the evening and better awake in the morning. It also strengthens the sense of balance.

A particularly positive effect has the third head position both on the emotional and on the mental level. It gives us comfort, security and the certainty that there is a force, whatever we want to call it, that carries, supports and loves us. Therefore, we can profitably use this position for the prevention and treatment of self-doubt, sadness, self-esteem crisis and depressive moods. It strengthens our self-esteem and gives us the certainty that everything is or will be good. We can experience what it feels like to be safe in God's love. This position helps with withdrawal symptoms and pain and, as the second head position, helps us remember our dreams better. Dreams are not foams but can help us grow and learn. This position helps with negative thoughts when we only see everything gray in gray. We experience more serenity and our creative energy is stimulated in the broadest sense.

At the spiritual level, in this position, we activate the third eye, the seat of holistic thinking and visions. In addition, our senses are sharpened and with it, for example, our ability of clairvoyance and precognition. This position also makes us more receptive to higher energy vibrations.

The Fourth Head Position Or Neck Position

With this position, we cover the thyroid gland on the physical level among other things. The thyroid influences the metabolism as well as numerous physical and mental processes through the secretion of the thyroid hormones T3 and T4. It is controlled by the hypothalamus and the pituitary gland, which produce the precursors of the thyroid hormones: TRH and TSH. Since the pituitary gland (pituitary gland) is very susceptible to stress, there may be under- or over-functioning of the thyroid in chronic stress.

Both are extremely unpleasant for those affected. In hypothyroidism, the whole metabolism is slowed down, causing constipation, weight gain, lethargy, and listlessness. In the case of an overactive thyroid, the opposite happens: the metabolism is accelerated, and people are usually thin, rather hyperactive, nervous, and prone to tantrums. With Reiki we bring the function of the thyroid into balance.

If you have more throat problems, you can do cause research with Reiki. We place our hands in the neck position and ask ourselves or our higher self: "Why do I have a sore throat now?" The cause may be, for example, that we swallowed negative feelings or did not use ourselves for people who were treated unfairly. With this position, we can dissolve energy blockages in the neck area. We activate the lymphatic pharyngeal ring, which serves as a filter on the one hand and on the other hand, transmits information about invading germs to the immune system so that it can provide the appropriate antibodies. With this position, we strengthen our immune system. Since it covers the carotid artery, this position is - in addition to the first front and the second back position is also recommended for heart problems such as angina pectoris and high blood pressure and has a favorable effect on the circulation. In addition, it helps therapeutically in stroke.

In the area of the neck position, we also find numerous lymph channels, which flow together in the mammary duct. Lymphatic fluid is an important bodily fluid that transports white blood cells to the sites of infection in the event of imminent danger, and slags from cell metabolism to the excretory organs. In terms of volume, it even surpasses the blood that flows through our bodies. It is not kept going by a pump, like the blood from the heart, but by muscle contractions, ie by movement. Since many people today do not move enough, the fourth head position - as well as the fourth front and back position - can make a decisive contribution to keeping the lymphatic fluid going.

For the emotional and mental level, this position is also very important. Many people, as I said, have become accustomed to swallowing negative feelings, but, of course, they are not out of the world and can lead to energy blockages in the neck, a lump in the throat or hoarseness. This position helps to dissolve the blockages in this area, allowing the energy to flow freely again. We do not necessarily need to let out so-called negative feelings like anger, resentment, and hostility, but we should not swallow them or try to keep them "under the carpet". With Reiki we can transform and dissolve them, so liberate them. The energy that we have previously used to keep such feelings in check is now available to us. We gain comfort, zest for life and respect for ourselves. The fourth head position also helps to calm the flow of thought and to articulate the thoughts more clearly, both in writing and orally. Now we are more ready to stand up to an opinion that we have formed for good reason, rather than direct ourselves like a flag in the wind to what is expected of us.

Also on the spiritual level, we benefit from the neck position. For example, because the throat chakra is the seat of expression, communication, relationships, truthfulness and the sense of justice, we will experience that our communication and relationships will become more authentic, honest and loving over time. Our love of truth and our sense of justice are also strengthened. It says, "God knows only the truth and the lie."

White lies are a human invention. "With Reiki, we'll get a sense that all the little insincerities are draining us of unnecessary energy. We are also more committed to people or animals who are treated unfairly and make us the lawyer of the weaker. Our creativity and productivity also benefit from this position. The throat chakra connects the lower chakras with the upper chakras and is therefore also called the needle eye of the energy and it's a power-generating energy center. So if you suffer from a lack of vitality and vital energy, you will benefit greatly from this position.

The Heart Position (First Front Position)

On the physical level, we cover the heart with this position and affect all heart problems favorably: nervous heart, angina pectoris, cardiac arrhythmias, high blood pressure, atherosclerosis with risk of heart attack. Low blood pressure is the only cardiac issue for which another position (additional position groin flexion) is more effective. The lungs are also in the range of the heart position. So if you have problems with your lungs and you may experience pneumonia or deep-seated bronchitis from time to time, you should hold this position more often and for a longer time. Lung problems can also be treated lying on one side by stretching the upper arm over the head to increase the "attack surface" and placing the other hand on the

62

lungs at the top, then at the bottom. Behind the breastbone lies the thymus gland. This is a small gland, which is responsible among other things for the growth of length. If she does not work well, dwarfism occurs. It used to be thought that the thymus gland stopped functioning at the end of puberty. But that's not correct.

Although the white blood cells are not formed, but trained, for their fight against viruses and bacteria. The thymus gland is, therefore, a kind of elite school. The T lymphocytes that are trained here have all the other white blood cells under them. With the first front position, we directly strengthen our immune system. In addition, the position has a favorable influence on the lymphatic system by preventing lymphatic blockages.

That the heart position is also important for the emotional level, is obvious. Not for nothing is the heart a symbol of love. However, from the heart center we develop a very special kind of love, namely unconditional or expectant love, even universal love that no object needs anymore. This is a very different love than the one sung in songs in which, for example, it means, "Do you love me? Do you really love me? Yes, then I love you too." This love is conditional and is turned on and off like a tap, depending on whether the other person reciprocates our love or not. With Reiki we are developing more and more unconditional love that is not tied to any conditions or expectations. Just as the rose gives off its scent, or the sun its warmth and its light, so too do we exude unconditional love. We need more of this love in our lives, and the world needs more of this energy.

When we perceive feelings in ourselves that are not in harmony with this high vibration of love, such as jealousy, anger, envy, hatred, or hostility, we simply place our hands in that position until those feelings change. For example, we find that our feelings were, for example, very positive for a person, that we liked or even loved that person, and that we eventually turned the tables on disappointment. And now we hate this person. But the opposite of love is not hate but, indifference. Reiki brings us back in touch with our original positive feelings and relieves stress. We learn not to resign, but to accept people and situations and to trust that ultimately everything will serve our best.

At the mental level also, we benefit from this position. Our thoughts become more harmonious, loving, constructive and benevolent. It's also easier for us to gather and concentrate.

At the spiritual level, over time, the heart position causes us to develop a more loving relationship with ourselves and others. We radiate more and more unconditional love from our heart center. This increased love ability is rewarded with happiness, harmony, joy in being, cosmic or unity consciousness, bliss, yes, ecstasy. If we have permanently achieved a unity consciousness, we can no longer argue with each other. To argue, to wage wars or to pollute the environment seems to you as absurd as if you wanted to cut off a piece of your own finger with full consciousness. No sensible person would come up with such an idea. It is also clear that as many people as possible must reach a cosmic or unity consciousness as soon as possible.

64

All our problems are related to the illusion that we are separate from others. In truth, we are all one. We are now experiencing this experience more and more often, and we can experience how we merge with others through our heart center, with humans, with animals and, for example, with the earth. So we feel more and more one and connected with all living things on this planet, and so we develop compassion.

The Second Front Position

In the second front position, the hands are below the chest, but still on the ribs. So we feel something hard under our fingers. This position is useful in the physical level for activating and promoting a healthy digestive system because here are important digestive organs, such as the stomach. There is a subtle balance in the stomach between the aggressive stomach acid (hydrochloric acid) and the sensitive gastric mucosa. Acid stoppers such as coffee, black tea or stress can damage the gastric mucosa. With this position we support the sensitive balance in the stomach. It is best to put your hands in this position before you eat so that the right amount of digestive juice can be produced. In the area of this position is also the upper part of the liver.

The liver is an important organ of detoxification. To neutralize the many environmental toxins we eat, drink, and breathe, she has to work overtime, so to speak. Therefore, the liver is slightly enlarged in many adults - a phenomenon that used to be known only by alcoholics. However, there are other important processes in the liver, such as the storage of vitamin K and the recycling of red blood cells. The spleen and gallbladder are also in the second front position.

The second front position is also very important for the emotional and mental levels. Many people swallow all kinds of negative emotions on a daily basis and this leads to energy blockages in the stomach. With this position, we dissolve these blockages, which can eventually lead to a nervous stomach, irritation of the gastric mucosa or even gastritis. Stress is an acid relaxer, and by relieving stress with Reiki and practicing with serenity, we spare our stomach. Fears, worries, and stress dissolve. Our thoughts become clearer and "friendlier", we are increasingly grateful for what we have instead of squinting for whatever we would like. In addition, we can collect thoughts easier.

On the spiritual level, we cover the solar plexus center or the sun mesh with this position - as well as with the third front and back position. This energy center is the seat of our self-esteem and self-esteem, which most people do not have enough of. This is especially true for older women. A lack of self-esteem is reflected in criticism towards yourself and others. If we have enough self-esteem, we can accept and appreciate others in their differentness. We do not feel threatened when someone has a different opinion than we do, but we see this as a way to broaden our horizons. With the second and third front positions, we develop more inner strength and strength, which we urgently need on our further spiritual journey. As a "reward," peace and cheerfulness that sets in without external cause are welcome.

66

The Third Front Position

With the third front position, we cover the small intestine, the transverse gut, the lower part of the liver and the pancreas on the physical level. This position is important for optimal digestion and can be used to prevent Diabetes II. In the small intestine the assimilation of the food takes place, in the large intestine the remains are thickened. The pancreas produces fat-breaking enzymes (lipases), regulates the sugar metabolism via insulin secretion and produces protein-splitting enzymes (proteases). With this position we support the pancreas in its important tasks. Our food is often low in enzyme after cooking, baking or roasting and contains too much sugar, so the pancreas often needs to work "overtime" and is therefore increased in most adults. The liver as a detoxification organ needs energetic support because it is strongly challenged by environmental toxins and food additives. With this Reiki position, we cover the lower part of the liver.

For the emotional and mental levels, the position is also important because it makes the feelings more harmonious. We no longer become hysterical, experiencing less anxiety and frustration and instead develop more self-esteem and greater self-esteem. The tendency to constantly criticize ourselves and others as well as our need to control or manipulate ourselves, others or situations. Our thoughts become much calmer and more harmonious.

On the spiritual level, with this position, we cover the solar plexus and charge our inner "battery" with life energy. Those who practice this position often learn to accept and let it happen. The inner strength and strength we are developing in this way is also important for our further spiritual path.

With the third front position, we are increasingly recognizing that we can no longer fight but let it happen, and that true strength is to practice devotion. Resistance creates suffering. By accepting situations and persons, including ourselves, space for change is created. Pressure creates only counter-pressure, which can manifest itself in the form of attack or flight. With this position we learn: We no longer need to fight negativity and thus become part of the negativity.

The Fourth Front Position

The fourth front position covers a number of organs on the physical level, namely the digestive organs of the large intestine, ureter, and bladder, as well as the genitals: uterus and ovaries in females, gonads and prostates in males. Therefore, this position is also helpful for good digestion and can be used both in constipation and in their "opposite", nervous diarrhea. It promotes detoxification processes and has also proven itself in chronic intestinal inflammations such as Crohn's disease or ulcerative colitis. As part of a full treatment you keep this position longer, because often complaints, such as migraine and headaches, with a poor digestive capacity together. Women who suffer from menstrual cramps should use this position for a period of one to two days before the expected onset of the disease, as this will relax the abdomen. For menopausal

68

symptoms this position helps as well as the fourth back position. The fertility of both sexes is favorably influenced by this position.

For the emotional and mental level also, this position is very important. We cover both the root or base center as well as the sacral chakra, which stands for sensuality, sexuality, creativity, and reproduction. We feel more grounded and better understood with responsibility and material. Over time, our existential fears, as well as the blockades on the level of feeling and understanding, disappear, manifesting themselves, for example, in closed-mindedness and prejudice. We get more flowing and become more open and tolerant towards the new. That makes us more adaptable in a positive sense. By activating the sacral chakra, we also get better in touch with our sexual needs and can better express these to our partner. In this way we promote our sexual health. Moreover, this position stimulates our creativity in the broadest sense. In other words, we are more creative with all our possibilities and more and more feel we have to determine our own lives instead of being lived "from outside". We are getting more and better ideas and more and more power to put at least part of them into action. This increases our self-esteem and self-worth.

On the spiritual level, we experience an expansion of consciousness and become more open to universal views that go beyond the borders of our individual interests.

The First Back Position

With the first back position, we can release neck tension on the physical level. Many people are constantly adopting a so-called "attentive attitude". That is, they unconsciously carry their chin up and pull their shoulders lightly. This attitude expresses, "Something could happen". Of course, something can always happen, but one thing is sure to happen when that attitude becomes a habit: the neck muscles are tense. If then sitting for hours in front of the computer, the TV or in the car, the same attitude is always added, one need not be surprised that the neck muscles in many are completely tense and so firm that they no longer head far left painless or turn right. Such people are usually mentally "rigid" and immobile, which can be expressed, for example, in fear of something new, intolerance or obsession with old age. With the first back position, we loosen the neck tension gradually and are thus also mentally flexible.

On the physical level, we also cover the spine with this position by sending light energy down the whole spine. I can highly recommend this position to anyone with back pain. Of course, if we have discomfort in the lumbar or sacral region, we can put our hands directly on the affected areas, with the palms facing out because that is more comfortable.

The first back position strengthens our nervous system and thus prevents its collapse. The spine can be thought of as a shaft through which a power cable passes: the spinal cord, from which nerve strands emerge, which then branch out and pull to the muscles and organs.

The first back position connects the heart chakra and throat chakra. That is, we increasingly feel the need to express the love that we develop from the heart chakra and to incorporate it into everything we do. There are many ways to express our love: through the tone of our voice, the vibration behind the words, and the way we do things, with the heart.

On the mental level, this position helps us to release stress more quickly and to relax more easily. Our thoughts become calmer and more stable.

At the spiritual level, we become more receptive to higher vibrations, experience more serenity, become more open-minded, and more open to the new. This keeps us mentally young.

The Second And The Fourth Back Position

The effect of these two positions is identical to the effects of the first and fourth front positions.

The Third Back Position

In the third back position, our hands are above the waist on the back. If you find this uncomfortable, you can also turn your hands so that your palms face outwards. We cover the kidneys on the physical level. The kidneys are vital organs. You are responsible for the water and mineral balance of the body as well as for the detoxification or purification of the blood. Given the environmental toxins and pollutants that we absorb with the breath, the drinking water, and various foods, we can imagine that the kidneys have to do an awful lot - and sometimes they fail. In Germany there are currently more than 35,000 people waiting for a donor kidney, and many more need to go to the hospital several times a week for bloodletting. By drinking plenty of still water - at least 1½ to 2 liters a day - and performing this position more often and for a longer period of time, we relieve our kidneys and strengthen them for their important tasks.

On the kidneys are the small adrenal glands, which are responsible for the release of the stress hormones epinephrine, norepinephrine, and cortisol - also called "corticosteroid hormones". These stress hormones have played an important role in evolutionary history. In stress situations, they made sure that our ancestors had all of their physical and mental strength in a matter of seconds and could either attack, defend or flee, perhaps to the next tree or cavern. Through this physical action, the adrenaline was broken down, and the hormone levels were balanced again.

Unlike our ancestors, today we suffer from constant stress, double or even triple workload, work stress or the stress of not having (paid and socially accepted) work. Even the noise level of a big city means stress for our nervous system, even if we no longer consciously perceive it. In rural areas, social control can create stress.

Most of all, the fatal thing about our present situation is that we can not vent our anger as a rule. Imagine, we are in the office and the boss criticizes us - wrongly, as we find. The natural reaction would be to take a gun, maybe a ruler, and attack the boss. Or flee the office and run three times around the block. Such behavior would be healthy, but it would make us lose our job. So we sit or stand and swallow our anger (or frustration). If two, three similar situations are added in the course of the day, we are latent at 180 in the evening. Then only one small thing needs to be added - the nursery looks chaotic, the washing up is not finished - and we are already getting out of our skin.

With the third back position, we ensure that our adrenals are not overly sensitive to any tiny stressors. In addition, with this as well as with all other positions of the full treatment, we ensure that all stress hormones are excreted as quickly as possible. Serene serenity and inner peace can only be achieved with a low adrenaline level. So if you do not know where to put your hands, I recommend you either "put them on your heart" - we all need more unconditional love - or in the third back position for more stress relief and serenity.

With the heart position, we can transform any kind of negativity and come into contact with our true nature. At the same time, we remind others of who they really are - their true, divine nature. Anyone who authenticly relieves stress with the third back position becomes a peacemaker. Imagine, there is a fight in the air, and you do not participate! The world needs much more of this kind of people. The world is waiting for you.

CHAPTER 10
THE GROUP TREATMENT

Group treatment is a very meditative experience and a wonderful opportunity to enjoy Reiki energy in a concentrated way. Everyone is treating each other in turn. As a result, the energy is not only added but also potentiated. This means that if we get group treatment from three people at the same time, that's the intensity of nine individual treatments. Of course, not everyone is treated for an hour. This is only the case with so-called »reiki marathons« that last for at least a whole day. But nevertheless, such a group treatment of perhaps twenty minutes is much more intensive than a one-hour individual treatment. Some say after a group treatment that they've been energizing for an entire week, and breakthroughs on both the physical and emotional levels are possible.

Additional Positions and Their Effects

In addition to the twelve items for full treatment, there are several additional items that are recommended for specific situations or diseases. As a rule, they are not applied on their own, but preferably as part of a full treatment. With the full treatment, we cover all possible causes, no matter at what level. In the acute case, such as nosebleeds or stress, we place our hands directly on the appropriate positions, but if possible, let others follow. In the case of accidents, for example, we hold our hands over the injured area, but then place it in the additional position of harmonizing it on the emotional level, in order to reassure the accident victim.

Additional Position - Groin Bends

This position helps with cold feet and very low blood pressure by not only stimulating the circulation of the legs but also gets the circulation going. Due to my very low blood pressure of 90 to 60, in the summer sometimes 90 to 40, I suffered in the past often from complaints such as dizziness or even syncope (small fainting). Since practicing this position, I have no such complaints anymore. It also helps with varicose veins, both prophylactically and therapeutically. Varicose veins are not only ugly but also health threatening because thrombosis can develop as a result. My identical twin sister has created a thick varicose vein in each of her four pregnancies. That's why I made sure to give myself the additional position groin bends almost every day during my pregnancies for five to ten minutes. With success! My third-year graduate sister also tried Reiki, and her varicose veins actually went down so much that they no longer need surgery. Therefore, if you already have varicose veins, you can still make significant improvements with Reiki.

Circulatory disorders of the legs are often referred to as "smoking legs" because above-average smokers are affected, but they can also occur in non-smokers. Those affected by the dreaded intermittent claudication can always walk a few steps without pain. When you're in a shopping mall, it's not so noticeable because you might think they are looking at the shop window displays. Diabetics often suffer from circulatory disorders of the legs associated with angioplasty. This means that they often no

76

longer perceive pain and often do not notice bruises or injuries at all or only too late. With the additional position groin flexion, we can help ourselves and others with such complaints.

Additional Position For Harmonization At The Mental Level

In this position, place one hand on the third eye and the other on the solar plexus above the navel. This position helps with stress, nervousness, anxiety, shock, and depression. It centers, calms and brightens the mood. I also recommend it for the aftercare and mental harmonization of accident victims. Of course, this position can also be used prophylactically, for example, if one tends to mood swings, and of course, it also works in children and animals. Children and animals not only process the stress that they cause, but also those from their environment, and they work intensely with the stress of their closest caregivers.

Additional Position For Energy Renewal

In this position, we place one hand above, the other below the navel, on the abdomen, covering the solar plexus, our "inner battery." If we were very active on the outer levels, eventually we may feel completely exhausted because our "battery" is empty. It takes at least five to ten minutes to recharge using this position, but it works. Many people drink coffee or coke when they are exhausted, but that is unhealthy in the long run. We "dope" ourselves and deceive ourselves about our real condition until eventually, nothing works and we suffer from burnout syndrome or total fatigue, often associated with anxiety or depression.

Even people with eating disorders benefit from this additional position. Often, not the stomach is empty, but the solar plexus, and we confuse the planes. Neither chocolate nor savory biscuits help against the lack of energy at the chakra level. So if you suddenly get hungry for salty or sweet food, even though you only had lunch one hour ago, maybe you'll try this position first. If the deficit is energetic, it helps you to balance it. If not, you can still eat something.

Additional Position Self-Esteem

One hand is in front, the other turned back from behind on the solar plexus center above the navel. This center is also the seat of our self-esteem and self-confidence. Due to their education - usually more criticism than praise - the vast majority of people have too little self-confidence. Women usually have even greater deficits than men, and the older they are, the more serious they become. People with poor self-esteem often suffer from criticism. On the other hand, the "solar plexus sandwich" helps because it gives us more and more of the inner strength that we need on our further spiritual path.

Additional Position Communication

One hand lies on the middle of the chest, that is, on the heart chakra, the other on the throat chakra. With this position, we connect these two energy centers and are increasingly in need of bringing out the unconditional love that we develop from the heart chakra. In other words, we do everything we do with love, and we also express that high vibration in our voice. Our communication becomes more authentic and at the same time more loving. Only when we signal to our counterpart with words and the vibration behind these words that we fundamentally value and accept him or her can legitimate criticism be accepted. It's simple: this position helps us to treat others the way we would like to be treated. When telephoning, a mutilated form of communication, it is important to place a hand either on the heart or the neck position. A good idea is to put a hand mirror next to the phone and to express your own facial expression control while speaking. When telephoning we should always smile. The others may not see that, but he feels it.

Additional Position "Loving Power"

In this position, one hand lies on the heart chakra, the other on the solar plexus. Napoleon, the powerful man, was often depicted with one hand on the solar plexus. For the saints found in Catholic churches, there is usually at least one hand on the heart chakra. In this additional position, the two energy centers are connected. Power and power (solar plexus) are good but much better in conjunction with the power of unconditional love that we develop from the heart chakra because power is "tamed" by the power of unconditional love. This is my favorite position in lectures and seminars. I stay centered and in the vibration of love, even when someone criticizes me.

Additional Position Ears

We put both hands on the ears, with either the index finger or the middle finger like a laser beam on the ear canal. However, it's not about touching the eardrum with your finger! We can apply this position to all ear problems, including tinnitus. So far, I had four tinnitus patients. In three, the tinnitus has completely disappeared, in one he has become weaker and occurs only rarely. This is a very good result compared to the achievements of conventional medicine, which tinnitus has recently been treated with psychotherapy because it has recognized the strong emotional component in this disease. In my experience, tinnitus patients are people who put themselves and others under pressure. One of my patients is a sales representative who originally worked 60 hours a week and who had a relationship with his marriage. Meanwhile, he has reduced his workload to 45 hours and ended his relationship. With Reiki, he realized that his lifestyle had caused his illness and he had to set other priorities.

This adjunct position also helps with middle ear infections, a problem that mainly affects children under the age of ten. It usually occurs between 19.00 and 20.00 in the evening, when the practice of the perhaps alternatively oriented pediatrician has long been closed. The emergency doctor, who can then be called, usually treated with antibiotics and rarely thinks to rebuild the damaged intestinal flora, for example with Symbioflor, so that the children have to suffer from bloating for weeks due to the disturbed intestinal flora. Concentrated action has been proven by my daughter, who has for a long time been dealing with middle ear infections: I make chamomile flowers hot in a pot without fat, put them in a cloth, for example, a tea towel, which I set with a rubber band, and place the "dumpling" as hot as possible on the affected ear. Then I fix the whole thing with a headband and put both hands on top of each other. In this way, we have still been able to avert the visit of the emergency doctor. I have nothing against emergency physicians. On the contrary, I admire their dedication, even at midnight and yet, it's nice to be able to deal with illnesses with Reiki and other alternative healing methods in a natural way.

When toddlers and babies scream when landing or taking off an airplane, you should give them the breast or the bottle. By sucking the pressure gradient is compensated and the ears do not hurt anymore. In addition, the additional position helps ears.

Additional Nosebleed Position

Nosebleeds are something that children often suffer from. Therefore, all those who deal with children should remember this additional position: one hand lies loosely on the bridge of the nose, the other on the back of the head, where otherwise one might lay down a cold washcloth. The patient sits best or he lies and has a thick pillow under his head. Then there is no danger that he will swallow the bloody fluid, which can lead to nausea. Often the nosebleeds stop after one or at the latest two minutes, even if it has dripped correctly before. Children who have learned Reiki are happy to help other children with nosebleeds, for example in kindergarten or school break.

My daughter has earned a reputation in elementary school as a little miracle healer. When a child took pills or used an ointment and she heard that she often asked, "Do not you have any strength in your hands?"

Additional Position Teeth / Jaw

If we have a toothache, we should definitely visit a dentist, because behind it may be a root infection. However, if we want to work prophylactically, we should focus on Reiki, for example on this additional position. We put our hands on the pine. This strengthens the gums and enamel, and that means periodontal and caries prophylaxis.

Tooth decay is no longer a problem for most adults, periodontitis very well. What use are the healthiest teeth, if they eventually fail, because the gums have developed back or even ignited? Many elderly people with periodontal disease give this treatment in the evening on television and are very satisfied with the result. While consulting a woman known to me, the dentist spoke of third teeth.
Nevertheless, after treating herself to Reiki for about four months and then calling the dentist again, he said, "I do not know what you've done in the meantime, but the subject is off the table."

CHAPTER 11
DECISION SUPPORT WITH REIKI

We live in a polar world and therefore we are constantly dealing with contradictions: negative-positive, yin-yang, love-hate, beautiful-ugly, cold hot and so on. Polar energies are always fragmentary and partial, never holistic, but with Reiki, we have an energy that is universal, holistic and non-polar - an energy that helps us to explore the inner connection behind the apparent opposites.

We can do the following exercise when it comes to making a decision, balancing alternatives, or dealing with issues involving affection or aversion. If we already have the second degree of authentic Reiki, we can focus energy on the theme during this exercise. If we already have the third degree, we can give ourselves or the subject the beginning of the exercise a mood and then, align the energy during the exercise accordingly.

The exercise takes about 20 minutes. During this time we should be undisturbed. We sit down or relax, close our eyes and place our hands in the first position. When we realize that we are very restless, we first place our hands on the third head position until our thoughts and feelings have calmed down.

Under the left hand, we imagine a color we do not like at all, maybe olive green or black. Under the right hand, we visualize a color we like very much, maybe a bright blue or sun yellow. Now we walk from the right hand to the left and slowly back, always back and forth. We observe whether the colors or our attitude towards them change. Then we move faster and faster from one hand to the other and keep watching what changes and what remains. We do not rate, but only observe.

Instead of using colors that we love or hate, we can experiment with other polarities as well. For example, we can imagine our dearest friend under one hand and the human being we least like under the other.

Maybe we want to move and have two apartments in view. Then we can imagine one another on one side and the other apartment on the other. Other polarities that we can work with are, for example, "qualities that I like about myself." And: "qualities that I do not like about myself." Or, "What I would like to do." And: "What prevents me from doing so".

Alternatively, we imagine a stressful situation under one hand that we may have just experienced or experienced in the past 24 hours, and go deep into the sense of tension and pressure without judging the situation itself. Then, under the other hand, we imagine a wonderful situation in which we once found ourselves, and in which we were quite alive and happy. When we have experienced this situation does not matter. We just go deep into the feeling of happiness and joy and then switch back to the hand with the stressful situation.

What has changed? We spend a few moments before turning our attention back to the hand where we have the happy experience. In this way, our attention moves from hand to hand several times. Then we let go of the attention and only feel the universal energy that builds up between the hands and the heart center.

Anyone who wants writes his observations in a "light diary". To lead such a diary I recommend to anyone who experiments with Reiki. You write your experiences into them without evaluating them or comparing them with others. This teaches the neutral inner observer, an important authority when it comes to growing into the consciousness of serenity and detaching oneself from identification with the mind.

CHAPTER 12
REIKI FOR CHILDREN AND ADOLESCENTS

Reiki is easy to learn, and I often give classes that allow elementary school children to participate. However, some children prefer to attend a "normal" class together with a parent or both parents. If children are still too small, I can give them photos of the four first-degree attunements from the effects. Even babies can benefit: the immune system is strengthened, the children sleep better and are mentally more balanced. Schoolchildren can concentrate better, are more motivated and self-confident, and learn better.

Reiki helps children build deep relationships with parents, siblings, pets, and nature, with growth at all levels and with the challenges of lifelong learning. Reiki already accompanies children in the womb of their mother, at birth and at every stage of their lives. Children need Reiki - and us! - at every stage of their development, even when they are already bigger.

Reiki is a wonderful way to maintain a bond of heart, a "dialogue without words" between parents and children, even in "stormy times" such as puberty. My son, now 18, wakes up forty minutes earlier each morning to get a Reiki treatment from me. In the morning, I "energize" both children, and when they write class papers or lectures, I direct energy. Even problems such as drug addiction, hyperactivity, and eating disorders can be successfully "circumvented" or transformed with Reiki because Reiki strengthens the self-confidence of children and adolescents.

When children find it odd that we suddenly keep our hands still instead of caressing them, we can simply stroke them in between to slowly get used to them. When children are very restless, we can just hold their hands over them while they sleep. Some smaller children do not like the first head position. If we notice, we just make the third head position a little longer instead. Children love to treat their parents and feel bigger and stronger. In many families, regular group treatments have become an important ritual.

In friendship with God of Neale Donald Walsch, we find valuable information for the education of our children. We should spend more time with our children and not pretend to have grown up with eleven. We should engage with their lives and care about them no matter how old they are. We are invited to speak to their teachers and make friends with their friends. God sharply penetrates us: "Claim your influence. Be really present in your life. Do not let them slip away from you. "What comes next corresponds to what neurologists like Professor Dr. Manfred Spitzer say: "Take a clear and distinct beachside point against violence and violent role models and force the cultural workers to a new ethic. Images teach faster and more formative than words. They create an ethic of nonviolence. Most importantly, banish the violence of your own life". In the eyes It is God's insanity to give your offspring a behavior that you should not copy, as you say. We even kill people to keep people from killing people. And the craziest insanity is to pretend that all this does not happen, and then wonder why your children are acting insane." In 80 percent of television programs, including public service programs, violence plays a role. On January 15, 2007, the newspaper said that two seventeen-year-olds stabbed a couple without a clear motive. Her favorite pastime: sitting at the computer and playing killer games.

Educating children is very nice, but sometimes very exhausting. When my son was 14, I made a fool of himself over his friends by secretly watching him behind the bushes and then letting me out because I thought he was smoking hashish. It was "just" a cigarette that went around for cost reasons. I did not necessarily make a name for myself with my son when I made him promise not to use illegal drugs by the time he graduated from high school, and then kept checking on that promise with drug testing. I gave him the driving license for that. After watching Professor Spitzer's film Caution Screen together, he brought Warcraft, the only computer game he threatened to become dependent on, to waste alone. I gave him a new value. Of course, although Reiki is not enough for a successful accompaniment of young people, it is important in my view to strengthen the inner bond with our children, however old they may be.

CHAPTER 13
REIKI FOR ANIMALS

The fate of animals is linked to our consciousness development. We have countless friends, at home or in the wild, who are excited about our energy and want to celebrate unity with us on the energetic level. In general, all nature is waiting for us to develop our consciousness. This transformation also transforms the animal kingdom, and lambs will be with the lions, as the Bible says.

Taking care of animals is a wonderful opportunity to expand the heart chakra and celebrate the unity of all life. Many people have learned that Reiki provides a depth of inner connection to animals they did not know before. With our Balinese cat Benita, I often did an eye meditation for half an hour or more: we were facing each other - they on my hand and my forearm - and looked into each other's eyes for a very long time. I sent her cosmic spirals. In doing so, we have merged into one being. The charming: Not only I felt that, but also Benita. This is a knowledge that has nothing to do with the mind. We now have a little cat. Kati is only four months old, and yesterday we shared unity consciousness for the first time. It was wonderful and I know that it was not the last experience of its kind.

Because most of the animals we can normally give Reiki to are smaller than us, we can afford to have fewer positions for them.

You will notice that some animals - some cats and dogs, for example - do not like the first head position. Just be flexible and give them the third head position as an alternative. If animals are injured or do not want direct contact, you can just hold your hands over them. For animals in the wild, you work with remote treatments, cosmic symbols or attunements.

With Reiki, we can strengthen the inner connection to all living beings. When we send energy to a pet or a wild animal, we often get deep insights into its nature and, when it is sick, into the nature of the illness or mental or physical crisis. With the "energetic look" that we get through Reiki, we grasp which animal species or individuals need our support especially intensively. Then we apply the remote treatment, as we have learned in the second degree, or make attunements, as you learn from the IIIA degree. Every year millions of lab animals, sometimes after untold suffering, give their lives for medical advancement. We can energetically support them too, as well as the animals in factory farming, which cramped their lives and which, except on the way to the slaughterhouse, do not see daylight in their short life, not to mention juicy pastures.

Yvonne Schiwalski from Heupelzen writes how she lost her extremely pronounced fear of wasps with Reiki: "Unnoticed by the mind, my behavior changed. I was really aware of this when I saw a wasp whirring around my nose when hanging out on the balcony and I did not flee back into the apartment in panic. I took a step back and just waited until she was gone. For most people a matter of course - for me a step forward!" She also writes about another experience with animals": Barbara told us in the seminar that children and animals for the heightened vibrations of Reiki are very sensitive. I can only confirm that.

For some time, more and more animals have deliberately been put into the service of humans. Whether it is dolphins that give severely disabled children the new quality of life and vitality; riding horses on which these children learn to trust basic trust, or dogs that bring light to old people's homes. Not only dolphins but also cats can help autistic children to escape. These animals, whether we know them or not, deserve our energetic support.

CHAPTER 14
REIKI WITH PLANTS

Like all living things, plants also react very positively to the light energy that we give them with Reiki. They grow better, vegetables and fruits taste better and mature sooner, flowers bloom longer and more luscious. If you only have indoor plants, you can handle the first ReikiGrad. We can treat individual plants and the irrigation water. We treat plants by first holding their hands around the roots or flower stems for a few minutes and then moving their hands upwards to the flowers and leaves. After such treatment, potted flowers bloom lusher and cut flowers last longer.

If you have a garden, you should consider getting the second degree, because, with the remote treatment, we can look after the whole garden, no matter how big it is. In my two organic gardens, I have made it a habit to hold seeds or seed potatoes in my hands for a few minutes before sowing them. I've found that the seeds are better off, make the potatoes better, and make the plants more resilient when supplied with cosmic energy as early as possible. We can also treat garden plants or trees by placing our hands around the plant or the tree trunk on the ground. For trees, we should put our hands around the trunk to energize the tree.

Dealing with plants, whether indoors or outdoors, is for me one of the most beautiful occupations there is. The color green nourishes our heart chakra, and by caring for something - whether animal or plant - we develop our heart center.

CHAPTER 15
REIKI AND HOLISTIC HEALTH

Reiki is the ideal remedy to not get sick and live long, with a high quality of life. It is an individual health system not only for healing but also for the prevention of diseases. Therefore, more and more Reiki courses are subsidized by health insurance companies. Reiki relieves stress and empowers us to cope better with stressful situations. In addition, it leads to more self-confidence, inner peace and happiness strengthens the immune system and activates the self-healing powers. When we practice Reiki, we will, from the inside out, tend towards healthier diets and discover a never experienced joy of movement.

With Reiki, it is possible to maintain the quality of life into old age. Reiki can also give us the experience that real peace does not depend on the condition of the body. The identification with the physical level is relaxed, and we realize that we are not bodies but have bodies. "Suffering comes from believing in patterns of thought that fool us, that we lack something." A person who does or meditates in Reiki learns to be an observer, whether his body is healthy or ill, Buddha suffered from food poisoning for six months before he died of it. It does not say that this disease did not cause him any pain, but the pain did not disturb the consciousness inside him. The body suffers, but there is no identification. This is the miracle.

Finally, with Reiki, we gradually lose the fear of death because we realize that the essence is immortal. Also, this knowledge improves our quality of life in old age, because only when we are no longer afraid of death, we can really enjoy our lives in every phase of life. When we are constantly afraid of losing something, it does not really belong to us. Of course, this also applies to material matters. Only when we are ready to surrender, we become owners. Miseries - whether they are stingy with money or love - are poor.

Although Western medicine has a mechanistic picture of man, we are not a machine, but multidimensional spiritual beings. Therefore, it is not enough to treat a diseased body part, because the ill part only shows that there are problems in the whole organism. If one symptom is gone, another can take its place. Health is not the absence of disease, but certain well-being, an oneness with existence.

To recognize one's own immortality means a great freedom - of death, illness and old age. Our true self remains untouched by the apparitions that come and go. We have an "inner health" just waiting to be discovered. Osho mentions four expressions of that true health within us: to be alert, to be harmonious, to be ecstatic and to be compassionate. Meditation or Reiki as a form of meditation can fulfill all four conditions. Ecstasy is the supreme joy, and compassion comes naturally. Researchers have found that young children who are already 18 months old are helpful and selfless, without expecting any personal benefit. This goodness has been lost to many adults.

Even Paracelsus called for a positive definition of the term health. He said, "Unless we know the state of inner harmony, we can only free you from your illness but the source of your health is inner harmony, but when we have freed you from one illness, you will immediately have another, for nothing has happened in relation to your inner harmony. In fact, it's necessary to support your inner harmony". Confucius had the idea of paying doctors to keep their patients healthy, not cure them. If the doctor is paid to cure you, he has an interest in keeping you ill. The more often you are ill, the better, and the more people are sick, the better. In ancient China, the doctor had to pay for all medicines and was responsible for all other expenses when his patient became ill. In addition, his income was reduced, because he obviously had not taken enough care of his patient. It worked for centuries, and both sides were satisfied.

It is also possible today to live a healthy life and even more: Radiant health is in our eyes our birthright. We just have to claim it - and do something for it. Health does not exist in commerce, it is fought for by way of life! Reiki is holistic, on all levels and causal. Over time, we literally become a new human being who, not least, has faith in God and in our hearts, as Dietrich Bonhoeffer puts it so beautifully:

"By gracious powers so wonderfully sheltered
we expect confidently, what may come.
God is with us in the evening and in the morning,
and certainly every new day. "

CHAPTER 16
SPIRITUAL HEALING

It is well known that the ancient sages taught that the generation of the elements is made as follows: each element dominates the other, stopping its development within a cycle that in turn generates the child element. This son begets the grandson. Thus each element is the mother of the one who follows it and the son of the one who precedes it.

They are called elementals:
Water - is associated with the Great Mother, birth and fertility. It is used in magical rituals to attract love, friendship, good luck, stability and healing.

Air - is associated with breathing, providing us with inspiration, thinking, speaking, singing, reading, praying.

Earth - is the element that generates life and then asks for it back. It is linked to progressivity, organization, responsibility and perseverance. It is physical reality, the altar of the Magician.

Fire - is the element that promotes transformation, passion, anger, strength, power, courage and purification. It is related to the realm of energy and power.

The cycle repeats itself in this order: Wood generates Fire; the fire the earth; the earth, the metal; the metal, the water; the water, the wood. This is the chain.

Meditation

Meditation is a spiritual practice. It leads to self-discovery, spiritual renewal, inner peace and balance between the various levels of the human being. This practice should be used systematically for preventive purposes. When we meditate, we are offering rest to our inner self. Physical rest is necessary, but the rest of our soul is paramount. We should practice meditation not only to cure some state generated by an imbalance, but also to prevent it from forming by cultivating the general harmony of our body and soul.

With your usual practice we will see significant changes in our intellectual performance, behavior, decreased anxiety, increased self-esteem, spontaneity, self-respect, ability for interpersonal contact, self- achievement, perception capacity, academic performance and a shorter recovery time from any stress (fatigue).

People who meditate habitually are clearer about deciding on serene behaviors and making themselves available to a better quality life through exercise, natural diet, cultivation of leisure, and better division and employment of their time.

These effects are just the opposite of what stress causes. The sense of inner peace and self-satisfaction brought about by meditation changes the biochemistry of the organism.

If we practice patiently in this way, gradually the distracting thoughts will cease and we will experience a sense of inner peace and relaxation. Much of our stress and tension comes from our own minds and many of the problems we face, including health, are caused or aggravated by this stress. If we do a simple breathing meditation for ten or fifteen minutes a day, we can reduce it.

Meditation leads us to experience a calm and spacious mind and many of our ordinary problems will disappear. This makes us better cope with difficult situations and, of course, we will feel warmer and more positive with others, thus improving our relationships.

We begin by calming our minds with breathing meditation and then move on to analytical and positioned meditations. Practicing in meditation will enable us to meditate regardless of what is happening around us.

Chakras

The word chakra comes from the Sanskrit language and means wheel or circle. They are the collection centers, stores and distributors of vital energy (prana) for our body. There are thousands of these force centers distributed throughout our body, interconnected by energy channels called nadis. In Sanskrit nadi means tube or vessel. The nadis form an energetic mesh that carries prana to all points of the body, which enables the performance of our vital functions which support our organism.

The chakras act as receivers, transformers and distributors of the various prana frequencies. They absorb vital energies from the cosmos and from the basic sources of every manifestation of life, transforming them into frequencies necessary for the maintenance and development of all human bodies, from the physical to the subtlest.

The chakras capture the vital energy, and the nadis distribute it. There is also the opposite movement, that is, our chakras radiate energy to the environment.

The chakras can suffer injuries such as obstructions and fissures, and can become misaligned, totally unbalancing a person. Reiki energy aligns and restores the balance of the chakras, bringing them into harmony with the cosmos and nature, thus enabling us to receive the vital energy we need.

7 Umbanda Lines

The spirit is recognized by seven rays, seven spiritual spheres, seven colors of the rainbow, and mainly by the seven main chakras. The Creator manifests Himself sevenfold to us, from the foundation of creation to the seven senses of life.

The seven senses and elements on which the seven lines of Umbanda rest are:

1. Coronary chakra - sense of faith

2. Front chakra - sense of knowledge

3. Laryngeal Chakra - sense of order / law

4. Heart chakra - sense of love

5. Splenic Chakra - sense of evolution

6. Umbilical chakra - sense of justice

7. Basic chakra - sense of generation

Each of them arises from the individuation of the Creator's seven maximal qualities in the creation of seven maximal deities.

These are the seven largest chakras and their natural vibration. As we ecarnate to learn and evolve, in each incarnation comes a new combination of Orixás in relation to the chakras.

The ancestral Orixás along with the recessive are the only ones who do not change from incarnation to incarnation being present in our coronal chakra.

AURA

The aura is an energy field that surrounds the physical body, protecting it as a sheath of light. This wrap can range from a few meters to something that cannot be measured, specifically in enlightened beings.

As a disciple you can measure the aura by visualizing it, by beings who have this ability, or through a physical process called Kirlian Photography. Although it bears this name, it is not a picture of the aura, but a holographic record recorded in an ordinary movie.

In addition to the extension, the aura also has color. These two properties define the state of physical and emotional health of a person. In the process of spiritual harassment, the aura and chakras are the targets.

Just as it acts on the chakras, Reiki also acts on the aura, restoring, strengthening, clearing and protecting.

Reiki is a part of each of us. It is part of our genetic heritage. One day was universal and should never have been lost. At the beginning of the planet's civilization, the children of civilization today known as Mu received training in Reiki I at the beginning of elementary school, in Reiki II during the age that corresponds to the second grade of regular education. Reiki III, the Master / Instructor, was required of educators and was available to anyone who wanted to receive it. When the people of the root culture left the land of Mu to colonize what today is Tibet and India, Reiki continued with them. The catastrophes that occurred on the planet, first destroying Mu and later Atlantis, produced various cultural conflicts, forcing the hand healing technique to be known to only a few. When, in the nineteenth century, Mikao Usui, Director of Doshisha University, Kyoto, Japan, Christian pastor, sought the origin of the healing method of Jesus and Buddha, he found it among the ancient remains of Shiva culture in the esoteric teachings of India. .

The Tuning

The learning Reiki healing technique is done in three levels, with a particular tuning in each of them.
Reiki I - The energy channels are opened and the disciple learns the basic positions of treatment in the physical body. It allows

you to apply energy to yourself and others. Receives the first symbol.

This symbol means the descent of Light, Power, and Energy. Pronounced it "chokurei ". It applies to blocked chakras, transmuting negative emotions, and filtering out the energies that pass through. It is used whenever the healer feels the need, mentalizing or drawing it by hand. One way or another, it must be "placed" three times by repeating the mantra (symbol name) It can also be projected large on the patient, and visualize him entering his physical and spiritual bodies.

Reiki II - In this attunement the disciple learns two other healing symbols.

The pronunciation is "sei re qui ". It is used to cure mental / emotional habits. Release conditionings, desires and feelings.

The distance healing symbol enables us to send healing energy to others at a distance. This symbol is also used for karmic release as it works the mental body.

We get used to recognizing time linearly, with beginning, middle and end. We must understand that from an energetic point of view time is composed of several layers that are interconnected, existing simultaneously. Thus a blockage generated in the past life gets stuck in our energy field until it is transmuted and turned into learning. This is the main function of Hon Sha Ze Sho Nen symbol.

Reiki III - This is the masters level. Both symbols are used in Master / Facilitator initiations.

In Traditional Reiki one receives the symbols through specific attunement. It may be in a preparation-coated ceremony, an appropriate place, which makes this moment very special, but it can also be quickly, without any apparatus.

Before starting Reiki healing treatment, anchoring is required and at its end, the disconnect.

Anchorage

Whatever kind of energy work we are going to do, we need to be solidly rooted with the earth. This is also true of Reiki.

The simplest way to ground ourselves is physical work.

Any kind of work, no matter what. Some types of sport, such as walking for example, as long as it makes us sweat, is a form of anchoring. Others, such as swimming, cycling, but it can also be sweeping the house, taking care of the plants. Physical exercise brings us back to the body, to the earth.

Finding our balance between heaven and earth is a wonderful experience.

A simple way to anchor is to lie on your back, completely stretched out on the dirt, sand or lawn ground. Imagine a kind of root, coming out of your hara, and penetrating deep into the earth. Try to feel the energy and nurturing force that emanates from the earth and enters you.

Seek anchoring in trees. These are concentrated energies that easily transfer to us. Many sit under their crowns and let themselves be charged with their energy without even knowingly knowing what they are doing. Having opportunity, hug a tree and ask her to give you the energy you need. You will immediately feel the strength it will give you. Don't forget to thank.

Meditate and anchor. Whenever it's going to be the Reiki Energy channel, empty your mind, anchor it, and start your work.

A quick form of anchoring we suggest now: standing, or sitting in a chair, with feet parallel, body relaxed. Put your hands on your hara (energy point three fingers below your belly button) and leave them there for at least ten minutes. Inhale and exhale deeply from your belly. Feel connected to your inner center and notice the energy of the earth rising within you until you reach your hara.

Disconnecting

After application blow or wash your hands. Use one of the four main elements of nature. Thank you for being a channel of Divine Light and only then the patient can say what he felt, if he wants.

It is not, therefore, a physical entity, and has its headquarters in the higher spiritual spheres. Performs functions of high relevance to the life of the planet and can be considered as the "internal government of the world ". It has many departments, such as Government (which oversees the executives of nations), Cultural, Scientific, Educational and Religious.

The destinies of the planet, therefore, are entrusted to this grand organization of Beings of Light who work, with greater love and dedication, for the good of our earth and its inhabitants. "

In the studies offered to us, I point out to the awakening of your interest, The Seven Rays and their Directors

First Ray - Blue Flame

MASTER ASSOCIATED - EL MORYA

Characteristics of people in tune with the First Ray:

Great action ability, unlimited energy, leadership.

Second Ray - Golden Flame

MASTER ASSOCIATED - CONFUSION

Characteristics of people in tune with the Second Ray:

Preachers, common sense, kindness, teaching with understanding.

Third Ray - Pink Flame

MASTER ASSOCIATED - ROWENA

Characteristics of people in tune with the Third Ray:

Fraternity with kindness and adoration, love of beauty.

Fourth Ray - White Flame

MASTER ASSOCIATED - SERAPHIS BEY

Characteristics of people in tune with the Fourth Ray:

Artists in general, perseverance, aesthetes.

Fifth Ray - Green Flame

MASTER ASSOCIATED - HILARION

Characteristics of people in tune with the Fifth Ray:

Doctors, nurses, scientists, healers, blessers, researchers.

Sixth Ray - Golden Ruby Flame MASTER ASCENTED NOTHING

Characteristics of people in tune with the Sixth Ray: People of great piety, priests, ministers, pastors.

Seventh Ray - Violet Flame
MASTER ASSOCIATED - SAINT GERMAIN
Characteristics of people in tune with the Seventh Ray: great love and work for personal, community and planetary freedom.
Say Good Morning, Friend

The best way there is to start one day is to give a sincere GOOD MORNING, FRIEND, aimed at the great friend we all have up there. He is so friendly, but so friendly, that he accepts to be called by a lot of names. They call him God, Alah, Ogun, Buddha, in short, every belief of the many in the world calls him a name. Calculate that even from Mbote Mondele I have heard him called him (that is, in Lingala, Good White. How? Where is Lingala spoken? Why ... in Congo-Africa. The important thing is never to forget Him, for He never Forget about us.

Sometimes we think that He is bad. That's when things don't go well for us, when we lose someone dear. But ... do you know the history of footprints in the sand? Yeah ... on those occasions when we thought we were abandoned, because there were only footprint marks ... It's because we were being carried ... not abandoned ... Think about it ... It's very simple to blame Him for our own mistakes ... or even things that happen to us through the mistakes of others. Take a good look and see. The fact that we are complaining is already a sign that we have the strength for something ... So, how about taking advantage of that strength that we have left to at least try to reverse the situation. Well, talking about the names with which we address Him ... I usually talk to Him, treating him by Buddy, or even Chefinho. Since our friendship dates back many years (and puts years into it!), I can have that intimacy. Well, children, for a change we hope that everyone, united, together at the same time holding hands and together in unison, will always have our well-directed thinking.

Things Of Ingratitude

When we suffer from an act of ingratitude, we are sometimes devastated, because we could never assume that someone who has always deserved our friendship and consideration could do so.

But if something can be a consolation, usually the "victor ", if that's what we can call someone who makes such a scam, ends up suffering more than their "victim ". Yes, when that person who could not understand us, realize the degree of bullshit committed, it will be late ... then, then, give value to those who had on your side.

Now that partner who defrauded us, who robbed us of what we had most importantly ... despite succeeding ... despite making a fortune ... is he at peace with his conscience?

Does he sink its head into the pillow and sleep in peace?

Maybe, but one day, the house goes down. Have no doubt, and I'm not talking about the "punishment of God," no. And I'm saying that someday this person will inevitably look back, and see that his whole success has simply begun ingloriously ... and that feeling is not very pleasant ... this idea that "I have no merit in this " already drove people to despair. Finally, let us not be tragic, or wish evil on anyone, but only that people become aware that dignity is too great a good to despise and think better before trying to rise, over the one who has always dedicated their friendship to them. .

Some Difficult Moments

It would be very nice and enjoyable if we had only moments in our life that were delightfully lived, whether in good company or even alone, provided they were lived with peace and tranquility. I believe that is the desire of any living being. Peace, health and tranquility.

However, we will always have to go through times when we will encounter some difficulty, or even many difficulties. It's inevitable. They even say it is the "spice of life ." These will be the times when we must make some decisions that will define our future, or even affect others' lives. Precisely for this reason we have to go carefully.

Generally, such important decisions should be well thought out in times of solitary meditation, for this is how we can best develop our thinking, but we should not hesitate to seek a second opinion if it is really complicated, especially with other lives on the

113

agenda. A reflection always imposes itself. Important decisions should never be made on impulse, as it will be a lot to play with luck, with the imponderable. One has to think, rethink, eventually listen, and then decide.

Sometimes the decision has to be immediate, we have to decide within minutes. It is always complicated to have to define a life in a short time. It can be a sudden trip. It can be a change of job, or life.

But perhaps we will not always be balanced, clear enough to define a situation that could turn doubt into certainty. If the dream will only continue to be dreamed, or will come true, in a delicious reality. If we will have moments of joy or sadness.

It is always better to take a moment to think.

Especially if our love life is at stake. Whether to start or end a relationship, it is very dangerous to do so in the heat of a passion, or an argument.

Before making a commitment, one has to see if there really is anything more than an ephemeral attraction, for a relationship could be for life. In the same way to end it, one has to weigh the pros and cons very well, to feel that there really is nothing else that justifies reconciliation.

It is always necessary to meditate, so that one does not stay after only regretting to have decided in a flash. When we can stop being loved, to be hated or vice versa. It all depends on the balance of our decision.

Making decisions in times of strong emotion can always be misleading. How many promises we make in our moments of passion? We are able to promise the world, to better live that moment, when we are living the madness of a love.

Promises we may not always keep, but that may affect our future, and the lives of those with us. These will be moments whose memories will be eternalized, and their consequences may haunt us for the rest of our lives.

On the other hand, how many loves end just because we couldn't measure the words in the light of a discussion. At a time when we send our love away. Then there may be regret. Maybe too late. For he took another way.

One of the things we complain about most is the misunderstanding of others. That no one understands us. We are always attentive, affectionate, etc. but we are not understood.

We complain that the person we care about doesn't understand us, no matter how hard we try to have a dialogue ... they can't understand us.
Now comes the fateful question. Is she not understanding us, or are we not being able to explain ourselves properly? We often hope that the people we address will have a perfect understanding of what we mean, but for one reason or another,

we cannot make ourselves understood. And we are hurt by the "misunderstanding" of others.

But the communication failure is ours. The most important point is to understand ourselves. Love each other. Get to know each other. Understand each other. This will enable us to be loved, known and understood.

Look at Richard Bach's genius thinking about this:

"For many years we hope to find someone who understands us, someone who accepts us as we are, who can offer us happiness despite hard trials. Just yesterday I discovered that this magical someone is the face we see in the mirror."

Of course not?

How can we be loved, loved, understood if even we can do it ourselves? The exercise of self-esteem is one of the most important things that exists. One of the best of these exercises is to look in the mirror and learn to like the person in front of you.

The face may not be exactly within what is meant by physical beauty, but it is OUR face, this is the one we have, and we will bear it for the rest of our lives (of course there is always the appeal of a plastic ... but that's another detail). And if we have to live with him, how about a peaceful coexistence? Find him handsome. Frankestein found himself. Why can't we find each other either?

The same about the body. If we don't like it, we can have a diet, or eat some more if we need to earn something else...

The important thing is to accept ourselves as we are, to like each other as we are. This will make it easier for us to begin to understand and love other people around us, and automatically we will be more easily understood and loved.

Love attracts love. Understanding attracts understanding. Good fluids attract good fluids. Positive energy attracts positive energy. Before someone argues that they love each other but find no boyfriend. It's all a matter of opportunity. You are on the right track. All that remains is to cross the fateful other half ... But keep loving yourself, that things can happen more easily. Insist, never give up. Know how to use your inner energy.

Experiences

The years go by ... Life goes by ... As the youth is left behind, we accumulate experience, as long as we know how to analyze the experiences lived, knowing how to separate what we did right or wrong.

Something I've always heard from my childhood as a child say: I would like to go back to my 20s, but with the life experience I have today ... Without a doubt, add to the vigor of youth, the experience that life brings in. his experience would be ideal. Too bad this is an impossible conjunction.

We need to learn from the mistakes made. This will form our experience baggage, which may allow us to have something to pass on to young people.

Life experience brings us a great advantage. If we know how to look back, realizing what the mistakes were made, we will not repeat them, as long as we know how to analyze them. Sometimes, the same error recurs. What if we do not always enjoy the lessons life gives us?

If we can pass on this experience to young people who are willing to accept it, we can even smooth out their path a little. We cannot and should not prevent them from making mistakes, what we can do is simply try to point them in a way. Show the options they will find ahead so that they decide what is best for them.

Since we have had the opportunity to use our free will, of course they have the right to do so and to make their own mistakes, to forge their own existence.

If they merely listen to the "voice of experience " without using their judgment, they will be amorphous creatures, unable to lead their own destiny.

We cannot "live life for them." We must let them live. Showing what exists, trying to alleviate difficulties, is one thing. Above all, we must let them think and come to their own conclusions. They will know that we are ready to help them whenever they need them and ask for help.

I found a very cool thought made by a boy who, like me, loved the Beattles and the Rolling Stones, but didn't pick up any machine gun. His weapon was the brain and a pen. His name was Victor Hugo and, among many other jewels, he gave us this:

"The fire is seen in the eyes of the young, but in the eyes of the old is the light."

See, the great sense that he put in the phrase: in the eyes of the old people sees the light. Light that can allow the experienced to light the way for the younger ones.

Light that can enable parents to show their children more clearly, but not to determine the path to follow. Lighten up for them to choose better. Light that is wisely used will allow younger people to make fewer mistakes. But they must be wrong, yes. If we get it wrong, we get here, why take that right out of them?

For if we want to make the way in their place, if we want to determine the way they should go, we will put out "the fire of their eyes." This fire so necessary for them to fight, try to win and reach their goals.

There is nothing better than being able to live in a pleasant, pleasant way, without many problems, without debt, with perfect health, many and good friendships ... and a few more things that do not occur to me now, but not always, and why not say, we can hardly reach this stage of total bliss. There is always a pen, or a bunch of them to disturb the context.

By the way we look at life, we will never be totally satisfied with our current situation, however good it may be.

And we are always waiting for help from someone above us. However, we may be able to make the task of the Friend a little easier. Just a little goodwill on our part, looking at some of the things we can do that can smooth our way.

Sometimes we have communication problems, we complain about not being well understood. It happens that we need to know how to talk to people, we must know clearly expose our ideas and ideals, trying, if appropriate, to shape them to the situation at the moment so that they are achievable. If we cannot communicate clearly, everything will be more difficult.

Often, the pursuit of success in life prevents us from living it properly, because in the desire to achieve certain status, we give up some pleasures, just dedicating ourselves to work, the desire to pursue success.

No doubt, it is important to get to the top, but in a rational way, without being forced to deprive ourselves of many pleasures, or worse yet, running over anyone in front of us, sometimes knocking down those who deserve our consideration.

We have to know how to use our inner energy in a more appropriate way, other than just looking for a certain situation, that makes us buy things we don't want, with the money we don't have, in order to show people we don't like, a person we really are not ...

In fact, it is much more important to do things that can give us pleasure than just things that, while improving our lives, can make us happy to live with pleasure, because in reality, nothing is funny if it is not. Good for the body, or even light for the spirit and pleasant for our hearts.

Using our energy to do something we really want and want to do, that makes us happy, and can help us make other people happy with our happiness.
We can't be in a hurry to get things done, we should try, even without waiting for success to come the first time. What we should always keep is a willingness to try again, and to do so, we must take care of our health so that we do not lack the energy to keep trying, with patience and determination.

We must have versatility to change our target if things get complicated, not getting discouraged by any mistakes or failures. We have to take advantage of them to learn not to repeat them.

To maintain our motivation, we must always have some dream to realize. Something to think about. A goal to be achieved.

What Will Be The Destination?

There is too much talk about things of Destiny, that our lives are governed by it, that our ways are traced when we are born. Well, if so, it would be enough for us to be born and sit waiting for Destiny to take charge of our lives. Of course we have to do our part ... we have to justify our passage through the world.

For this, there is our free will, which allows us to modify the Destiny. We simply cannot wait for things to happen and that is where the problems begin, for always in our life options will emerge. Life will set us before some paths to choose.

Which one to follow? If we have the intuition to take the most exact path, we can say that Fate has reserved for us good things.

However, if we choose the other side, we will complain that Fate has been bitter to us. Was it really ungrateful Destiny, or could we not choose? At the time of choice, we decided to choose a path that was not consistent with our real abilities or needs.

By the way, there's a quote from Shakespeare, which comes in handy on the subject.

"It's often the traitorous doubts that make us lose the good that ours might be, if the fear of trying didn't exist... "

This is exactly where the crux of the problem lies. Often, among the options that lie ahead, one seems to be the most difficult. Sometimes it is best suited for us. But it is complicated. Doubts us doubt about whether or not we can get it done. So we set it aside, trying other, easier things.

We often miss great opportunities because we lack the courage to make the right decision. For wrongly assessing the causes and consequences.

This applies to life itself as well as to romantic life. Love issues have always been a great source of doubt. How many times do we find ourselves at the difficult crossroads, not knowing if we continue with the love we have, or if we move to another, which seems more certain, more tempting...

Here, then, there is no magic formula to indicate the way ... it's all a matter of trying d escobrir "What we reserve the Destination."

Any of them may be the right choice ... or not. In that case, we will only have to rely on intuition and wisely use free will for the right choice, by weighing the possibilities, the pros and cons of the options that exist, for it is often our life that is deciding.

We have to know how to find our destiny. The only way I recommend is reflection. Never make any serious decisions in the heat of an argument at a time of great passion.

Decisive decisions always require deep and thoughtful analysis. Destiny often depends on a single word. Think carefully before you say it.

Eternal Dissatisfaction

There are people who go through life without ever being able to find happiness because they are never satisfied with what they have achieved in life.

Of course ambition is inherent in human beings. Of course, it is always lawful to wish to improve your living conditions. Of course, we should not just conform to what we have, and passively accept everything with a simple, conformist "It's destiny...".

But one must also consider that this ambition must be well directed. It is lawful to wish for improvements in our lives and to work for them.

However, we must always bear in mind that what we have already achieved has its merit, and so must be considered.

We should be pleased to see what we have already achieved and keep looking for new goals.

I agree with the saying: I don't have everything I love, but I love everything I have...

However, if we are in a state of permanent discontent, in addition to failing to achieve such happiness, we will also be disturbing those who live by our side. Nothing satisfies us.
In all we see defect. Nothing is done as we please. And things are not quite like that. If we can have some stability, that will not

be all right. The problem is that there is no definite goal, no goal to be achieved.

This situation simply does not serve us, and needs to be changed.

But ... what change would that be? You cannot define what needs to be changed. But it has to be changed. As it is, it is not good. There is no definite goal. You don't know what you want. But it is not good. Nothing is fine.

Be dissatisfaction with the financial situation, it could be better, but ... could you like? It is unknown ... But it should be better. Be it because your spouse doesn't give you the proper attention. What attentions are you complaining about? Attention, why ... You need to improve the treatment. What is the point claimed? Where is the fault? It's in your way of treating me ... But it is not defined what the change claimed.

Simply dissatisfaction exists, complicating the family relationship.
This also occurs in relations between parents and children, always causing mismatches that could be better resolved if there were dialogue.
The important thing is to have communication between people.

There needs to be understanding from part to part and that's kind of complicated, because this indefinite dissatisfaction is interpreted as a pretext for fights. It really is complicated for those who are the dissatisfied agent, because they cannot define themselves, as well as for the other side, which is kind of lost, not knowing what action to take.

For both sides, the only possible suggestion is a reassessment of the case, trying to figure out the best way to reach a consensus.

Tackling The Problems

Often, as we begin to encounter setbacks in our path, we begin to give up plans, dreams, and even living, just for fear of facing the beasts head on.

Let's look at a very beautiful message that says:
"The spiritual journey is to continually fall on your face, get up, shake off the dust, look shyly at GOD, and take another step."
What can be extracted, in practical terms, is that when we encounter an obstacle in our walk, we should not give up in front of it, but look for a way around it. We have to wisely use our inner energy accordingly.

Often problems arise in our relationship. If we simply adopt the ostrich technique and run away from it, the tendency is for it to grow bigger and bigger. However, if we seek, together with our partnership, to find a solution, this problem can be circumvented, especially if it is something related to the relationship itself.
How often do small doubts arise, which, if left unanswered, reach huge proportions, and the whole thing is harder to resolve.

Getting into the topic of marital, extramarital, intersexual, homosexual, and a few other "woes" out there, we find that a lot happens because people refuse to face certain problems caused

126

by age, the routine of a long life, preferring to run away in a way that sometimes becomes cowardly.

Other times the thing starts when the "light" that used to turn on at the simple contact of the bodies, begins to diminish, almost extinguishing ... So what? This diminution of sexual interest can have many reasons, without necessarily signifying the end of love between them. There may be some clinical factor. Then we should consult a doctor.

It can be just a burnout for many years of living, or even a consequence of the way of life. Due to professional demands, personal contact begins to diminish. This does not always cause loss of sexual interest, but causes a cooling. That old headache problem today, "I'm tired" tomorrow ... and it gets cold.

It's time not to run away from the problem, or look for "other ways " to test the degree of sexual attraction or potency that still exists ... It's time, yes, to face the issue, not to be afraid to face the dialogue ahead forward. It's time to look for alternative paths.

See what is the best way to come up with a solution. Even if things happened ... Let's get up, shake off the dust, and go around. We have our inner energy. Let's know how to use it.

...AND LIFE GOES ON

How many times do we have to reformulate plans, modify certain things in our life? And in order for these facts not to shake us in a hopeless way, we need to be prepared for the many possibilities life offers us.

A long cherished dream, for example. How many times have we imagined something we longed for? We get to see him close, almost realized. We get to taste it on the tip of the tongue, but some random circumstance, sometimes a misunderstanding, ends up knocking the castle that was almost ready.

At such times, we must be strong to bear the brunt, know how to react to the difficulty, and not let ourselves be drawn, seeking strength in our spiritual reserves, always bearing in mind that what has not been done now can be achieved at another time, just by Let us not be overwhelmed by discouragement at the impossibility of the moment.

It becomes necessary to show ourselves that we are able to withstand the misfortunes of life, always relying on our ability to fight. We must simply make each difficulty a step for the climb to which we are determined. We cannot simply give up on everything. It's a ball forward. ...And life goes on.

We must not forget that if Life puts stones in our path, it is certainly up to us to stumble or use them to better pave the way. We just need to know how to use our creativity and our inner energy.

Living The Life

Undoubtedly, we always have to look to the future, to try to guide our destiny in the best way possible, not forgetting to live the present as intensely as possible, even because we can never know how much future time we have left, be it 1 minute, 1 hour, 1 or more years, which is why it is very important to enjoy every moment and live it as intensely as possible.

The past is over, but it should not be forgotten. We should always take a look back. Whether to find some parameter for what is happening at the moment, or to see the mistakes made and not repeat them again.

We often face similar situations to those already experienced. It is interesting to take advantage of our experience to better understand what action to take. Take advantage of past mistakes or successes to confirm or change present situations. It's a way of understanding life.

Looking to the future, making plans to live it better, but without giving up the right to enjoy the present moment, which is actually the present to be unwrapped.

Trying to live in the present moment without attaching too much to the past. Many cease to live today, only evoking either the glories or the defeats that have already occurred. Well ... that's already behind us. And it is forward that one walks...

Pure Energy

Pure energy,

Spark of the Creator,

Purple cover,

Send your love,

Faith of the Inner Light.

Energy

Internal force

Pure energy, love

Acts on the body

Treat the spirit

Transmitting light, heat

Force of The Universe

I am ray of light,

I am from within,

I am peace I am love,

A part of the force,

Ruling Universes.

Flying

No obstacles

Make me give up nothing

I leave with desire

And flying through infinity

Better Days Will Come

Every day is always a day ... Yesterday is over ... Tomorrow has not come yet ... We have to face today, which should be worse ... than tomorrow, but better than yesterday. So let's go to him.

Today has started well. After all, we wake up, and if we wake up, it is because we are alive. And does anyone want to feel better than to be alive? Problems exist, always existed, and always will exist. And they must be resolved, or postponed, if the solution is too complicated, which depends on life circumstances. What counts is that pleasant feeling of feeling alive. Open your eyes, look in the mirror and be able to say "I love you, man." After that, the day will be perfect.

I think that really the best thing about positive thinking is the best thing to do, but we should be aware that this is not enough, because there is no point in having positive thinking if the desired things are far beyond the possibilities and we must also be realistic to make a parameter between the desired and the achievable.

It is important to know how to love what you get. There are many people who fight, fight, to achieve a goal, and then look at what they have achieved and exclaim: Wow ... so much struggle for that?

There is no point in setting unreachable goals, and then lamenting that you have no luck in life and that God has forsaken you, when, in fact, there was misdirected planning and God is not to blame for the nonsense we do. Therefore, the most important thing is to plan our actions.

When the motivation that leads you to this knowledge is there to help yourself and others. The Reiki Vital Energy will flow in the desired way if you take responsibility for your own well being. We must have the firm conviction that, as a recipient of the Greater Energy, we are the creators of our health and our happiness. Forget the ego. Surrender to the Higher Power that is your true Self.

At various times in our lives we are called to know our true nature. They are called Rites of Passage.
When we are driven by our Inner Self to the need to know a healing art like Reiki, we are being called inward to really know what we are.

Recognize, remember, for deep inside we know who we are.

Reiki initiation will be like a milestone that will accentuate our Rite of Passage, which will put us in touch with our origin. When we can get rid of the suffering of disease, when we can get rid of ego and mental confusion, we will have Peace.

Reiki is the life force of the universe. By accessing this knowledge we will be giving back to ourselves that we already are.

And as we recognize each other, we will then realize that we are Reiki itself.

As you assimilate this truth, you will find that there are no Reiki healers, just as there are no Reiki masters. When we heal with Reiki, we are opening to simply being a channel for the transmission of Greater Energy, Universal Vital Energy.

Similarly, when we teach the Reiki healing technique, we are acting as a simple mirror that will reflect to the student their true self. In both situations, what acts is the Greater Energy, not the ego of the student or the teacher. Humility is the achievable quality.

In this Rite of Passage, which is acting on you in the now, it was your Inner Master who informed you that you were ready to communicate your own wisdom.

Master and disciple are not separate, for we are ONE. It is right for the disciple to respect the master. He too must respect the disciple. Only then can there be a meeting of mind and heart.

As a Mayan greeting says "In Lake'ch" - "I am another you."

An old saying and wise saying goes, "healing begins at home." If we have a real desire to heal others, we must first heal ourselves.

The first step will be to free ourselves from limitations. We have been used to believing that we are limited. The collective unconscious is too castrating for both mind and body. We have been trained to accept that "having" is better than "giving." At this time in which we live, we are all conditioned to accumulate and retain accumulated possessions ... until death do us part. We participate in a cultural group where we learn that we can only give what we already have.

With the systematic practice of Reiki we realize that we are not limited. We realize that the universe gives us abundantly what we need. All we have to do is access. And with that, we become more generous. Thus the "I" disappears to give way to the "we". As we access Reiki healing, we realize that we are not lonely. The transfer of this Energy will always be from heart to heart.

Are you motivated to access Reiki? Create situations that feed this motivation. Everyday life with its troubles may divert them from this focus. This need for bestowal and freedom comes like a spark. And it has to be nourished, for it can be stifled by the illusory struggle for survival.

The first step will be to meditate. We have to conquer a space in our life, other than diving into the "have ". We return to our interior, and in solitude seek the "being ". Finding it will give you access to freedom, and may be the bestowal channel of Reiki energy.

For thirty minutes write your feel, damage sequence in the sentence we will put below. Do not exceed 30 minutes. Complete the sentence if time is up.

"My true wish in life is ....
....

134

....

....

...."

We know the first step. Let's go to the second.

Meditate, empty the mind, and now is the time to write.

It is important that you write without stopping whatever comes to mind. Without censoring or criticizing. Put your thoughts on and on for 30 minutes. Put it all out. Don't worry about aesthetics, nexus, and beauty. The words are within you as are the images. If memories come that hurt, scrutinize those memories, describing details. For example what clothes I was wearing, if your hair was long ... Don't worry about being whole, correct. Write everything inside you. If they are happy events, likewise, detail.

Follow the sentence below. Do not exceed 30 minutes. Complete the sentence if time is up. Do this in this email and return it to us, please.

"My   true   desire   in   life   is

....

....

....

....

....

....

....

....

...."

In so far as that we let them pass without clinging, we are gaining our freedom, and with it our peace and happiness.

We happen to feel that spiritual practice becomes a heavy burden to bear. This feeling is a clear indication that we forget to forget the ego. This ego rebels because it does not accept something over which it has no dominion.

Joy and pleasure in any activity you pursue is the right path, the one to go. We are all tired of our obligations, such as "do this" or "don't do that."

The proposal now is to find out what truly LOVE means to us. Emptying the trash can that is our mind is the most effective way to realize that in the end we are not our memories. Expressing what we feel right now will give us the freedom to follow the flow of life rather than block it even unconsciously.

Meditate, Empty The Mind, And Now Is The Time To Write

For thirty minutes write your feeling, following the sentence we put below. Do not exceed 30 minutes. Complete the sentence if time runs out

"For the lifetime I believe I will still have in this plan my wish is

....

....

....

....

....

....

...."

When we focus on the desire of a personal object or on a specific spiritual path we have to make a commitment. Commitment is not an obligation to anything or anyone but ourselves.

We must commit ourselves to the truth, the light of our inner wisdom. Decide what we really want, and commit to achieving the goal.

By making a commitment to Vital Energy we will be freeing ourselves from all doubts of who we really are.

We do not need to express our commitment, but it will be clearly perceived, for peace will reside in us and it will be spread among those who live with us.

It will happen that at some stage there will be a decrease in enthusiasm for Reiki, and it is normal for this to happen.

Hidden feelings will appear, and we will have to face them.

It would be like a purification process.

If we are clear about our commitment to accept things and events as they present themselves, we will more easily get rid of them.

Meditate, empty the mind, and now is the time to write.

For thirty minutes write your feeling, following the sentence we put below. Do not exceed 30 minutes. Complete the sentence if time is up.

"For the lifetime I believe I will still have this plan of mine wish is

....

....

. ..."

Only an energy can set us free, and this energy is the LOVE. When we fall into the truth that we are the energy of love, we are free from any other feelings that we want to embrace.

Reiki is the energy of love. As we learn to deal with this energy, we will be learning to deal with ourselves.

When we heal by Reiki healing energy, we are healing through the energy of love. When we are healed by the Reiki healing energy, we are healed in the love that is our essence.

There is no reference to what I say in the romantic notion of love, which we have learned to deal with wrongly, since this experience can always bring fear. The ego is afraid of love. Fear of losing control power. If the ego is conditioned to fear, it will respond according to what we have kept negative in our memory.

Meditate, empty the mind, and now is the time to write.

For thirty minutes write your feeling, following the sentence that I will put below. Do not exceed 30 minutes. Complete the sentence if time is up.

"For the lifetime I believe I will still have this plan of mine is

....

....

...."

The love leaves us vulnerable. We need, we want it, but we're afraid of your nearness. These are the memories we carry from childhood and even from other lives.

The fear of suffering causes us to turn love away from us, and we lose our taste for life, but deep down we know what we are. Our heart continues to emit the energy of love and we suffer. And we get anxious, feeling incomplete. Our ego can never control our hearts.

138

In its essence Reiki is a means by which we can return to ourselves what we already are: the expression of Love.

Meditate, empty the mind, and now is the time to write.

For thirty minutes write your feeling, following the sentence we put below. Do not exceed 30 minutes. Complete the sentence if time is up.

"I want love to manifest in me in the form of

....

....

....

....

...."

Humans we are creatures intensely sexual. We are the only mammals on the planet where sex is a gesture of intimacy and affection. This would be unquestionable proof of the spiritual dimension of human sexuality.

We have a distorted picture of sexuality, portrayed by its insistence on being tied to violence, rape and exploitation. It is necessary to understand that it is not her, sexuality, the error factor, but the power play superimposed on sex. We are responsible when we let ourselves control.

Reiki restores our bond with the energy of Love that we are. It is necessary for this that we are open to the universe that it will give us something that will far surpass our imagination.

Freedom, equality, justice and love can only be perceived and felt. They are born straight from the energy we are. If we know and accept it, it will happen.

Meditate, empty the mind, and now is the time to write.

For thirty minutes write your feeling, following the sentence we put below. Do not exceed 30 minutes. Complete the sentence if time is up.

"I have restrictions on demonstrating the love I feel because

....

....

...."

The world is a reflection of our consciousness. Being this true premise, consciousness is what we most lack. And along with that we still have a bad habit of judging ourselves and everything around us, without knowing how to firmly measure what these things or people are.

It would be best to recognize that we live most of the time oblivious to what is happening. We are conditioned to accept facts without even being aware of the air we breathe. We are not present in the Now. We do not have this awareness. We bring back what is past and project it forward without realizing the Now.

When we gain real awareness and are willing to feel in the Now, we will have the consequence of placing real value on our most precious possession: Life.

Our health and sanity now have more value than the outward concerns and conditioning imposed by the society of which we are a part.

As we exercise in feeling negative feelings and exploiting them, we will realize that it is all part of a great web where there is not just one culprit and only one innocent. Life will always present itself in a balanced way, based on respect and freedom. It is the exercise of our free will that will lead us to the path that may cause pain or happiness. It is a personal choice. Consciously personal.

Reiki heals by quieting the mind and raising the Life Force Energy. And it takes awareness to realize that. The motivation for learning and practicing Reiki is to eliminate an emotional or physical imbalance.

By the time we are determined to do so, we are already dropping unconsciousness and taking possession of our own lives, no longer allowing external factors to command it.

As we systematically practice Reiki we will eventually realize that the game of life is not something with its own substance, and we will then play it joyfully, for we will shape it as our consciousness determines.

Meditate, empty the mind, and now is the time to write.

For thirty minutes write your feeling, following the sentence we put below. Do not exceed 30 minutes. Complete the sentence if time is up.

"I   am   fully   aware   that
....
....
...."

We understand how to activate the power of healing in our body. No disease, be it material, emotional or spiritual, can be cured by a healer, by a medicine we take. It will always be repaired by the body itself.

There are several ways to activate the healing power of our body. The simplest and therefore the most important is your desire to become healthy. We bond with our complaints, with our pains.

The first step is to distance yourself intellectually and emotionally from "your" illness.

No more calling it "my headache", "my depression", "my knee pain".

We have to be fully aware that we are a Divine Spark. If we can direct our attention and take this spark of pain and bring it into the divine, we have come a long way toward health.

The flow of energy we absorb in making this spiritual self-affirmation is intense, and we can use it to heal our physical body.

We should always observe our body and listen to its desires. Over the years, we have gained the advantage of our body and mind becoming more sensitive and receptive.

Always remember that as Reikians, you should give your body a high quality slack daily. Relaxation is very important, but meditation is essential. While the relaxation rests body and mind, meditation relaxes the soul.

After meditation, make it a habit to apply Reiki to yourself. The internal circulation of Reiki energy will be intensified with initiation into Reiki. However, our ability to absorb the energy of the cosmos will also be increased. Reiki will affect us from all sides, inside and out. The flow of energy becomes stronger with practice as the Reiki channel becomes "clean".

What we ask today is that as you meditate ask yourself this question: WHO AM I?

Now write how you recognize yourself.

I   am...

....

Applying Reiki Energy In Yourself

When you undergo a treatment with Reiki participated of the discovery of healing and balancing through the direct bond we have established with our being.

With the practice of Reiki we reverse the tendency to systematically move away from our origin.

Reiki heals us deep within our being, gently, without undue imposition. As we open to feel the Force of Vital Energy, we feel more unified, more alive.

We will now begin treatment with Reiki Healing Energy.

Remember that to start your day and before you fall asleep at the end of it, you must meditate. Do meditation as usual practice in your life.

When positioning your hands to apply Reiki energy, let them relax. There is no need to touch your hands. Leave them 10 cm above the application site.

Reiki is a loving and conscious touch. Each position should take an average of 2-3 minutes. But be prepared for more as you may "feel" the need for some part of your body to need more energy. To start the Reiki application you will have to mind a White Light coming towards your head (coronary chakra) and entering it. You will have to be sitting or lying down.

Then make the applications and describe your feeling. With the consistency of the application you will notice differences. As long as you feel your warm palms remain in position, as this "point" needs healing energy.

First position: cover your eyes with your palms.

Second position: Cover your temples with your hands.

Third position: Cover the ears.

Fourth position: Cover the occipital lobes with your hands (small bulge at the base of the skull).

Fifth position: Put your hands on your throat.

Sixth position: In the previous position we had our hands on our throats. Slide one of them into the small concavity below the trachea. The other hand is placed just below the first, at the point between the thyroid and the heart.

Seventh position: covering the heart.

Eighth Position: Lower your hands until you place them above the solar plexus (just below the heart).
Ninth Position: Cover the four corners of the chest, placing one hand just to the right of the solar plexus and the other under the lower ribs.

Tenth position: Place one hand over the navel and the other immediately below it.

Eleventh position: For women: arrange your V-palms pointing at each other and touching the top of the pubic bone with your fingertips. For men: Cover the genitals with your hands.

Twelfth position: Cover your knees with your hands.

144

Thirteenth position: Put your hands on each leg and ankle.

Fourteenth position: Place your hands on the foot and sole of the foot.

Fifteenth position: put your hands on the soles of your feet.

Complete the entire Reiki Energy application sequence on yourself.
Describe the flow of energy in each of them:

....

....

....

....

....

....

....

Applying Reiki Energy To Another Person
The following will put the positions for Reiki in another person. However, it is worth repeating the following observations:

1 - Never apply Reiki without proper permission, as we can never hurt anyone's free will.

2 - Never deny applying Reiki when prompted.

3 - Don't be afraid to do the application. It will not be you who will be energizing the person. You are just a "channel" through

which Reiki Energy flows. Who is actually applying is your Inner Master, your Reiki Guide.

4 - The positions are as below, but if your hands decide to go to points other than this, let it flow because you are just a channel.

5 - Apply Reiki preferably in a calm place, in low light, soft music, light perfume incense. Doing so will not be a more effective channel, it will only provide better relaxation to the person to whom you are applying.

6 - If possible decorate the chakra and the basic reference of the physical ailments that they attack, as described below.

7 - If the person you are applying Reiki to wants to talk to, kindly ask them to be quiet, and after the conversation they can talk freely.

Welcome to the magical world of Unconditional Love healing
These positions need to be applied on others.

First Position: Standing or sitting behind the other's head, place your fingertips over the bony structure under the eyes. The thumbs are side by side, covering the eyebrows. The indicators a little apart from the nostrils. No need to put your hands on the person. Leave them about 10 cm apart.
This position relieves eye strain and provides overall relaxation. Ideal to relieve stress. All positions in the head treat the pineal and pituitary glands.

Second position: Cover the temples with your hands. Touch the temples gently but firmly.
This position relieves tension in the group of muscles that radiates from the jaw.

Third position: cover your ears with your hands. Be gentle so that the other does not feel energetically invaded. In a few minutes he will feel a deep relaxation, because in treating the ears, in fact will be treating the whole body, because the many energetic points located in it connect to all major channels and regions of the body.

Fourth position: Cover your two occipital lobes with your hands, "hooking" your fingertips to the ends of the skull near your neck and your hands are relaxed. This position releases the tensions around the head.

Fifth position: Be very careful when placing your hands in this position. Do not touch the person. This position is for treating throat problems, and the like.

Sixth position: one hand on the small concavity below the trachea. The other at the midpoint between the thyroid and the heart. Strengthens cellular metabolism and tones circulation.

Seventh position: covering the heart.
This position deals with complex rejection and resistance to love. Also treats any heart problem (physical)

Eighth Position: Place your hands just below the heart.

This position relieves stomach pain and nervous tension. In the energetic plane it helps in the resolution of questions related to wisdom and power.

Ninth position: covering the liver and gallbladder.

Collaborates with the general detoxification of the body. Whenever you feel the person is irritated, you should apply in this position.

Tenth position: one hand on the navel and the other just below it.

As in the heart, it is depression in this area, because depression is the repression of various feelings. It is also indicated for any digestive problem. It also balances sexual disharmonies.

Eleventh position: hands on knees.

The knees represent the fear of change, including the fear of physical death and the death of the ego.

Twelfth position: one hand on the knee and the other on the ankle.

Thirteenth position: ankles.

Fourteenth position: hand on each foot.

Treating the feet will be dealing with various points throughout the body.

Fifteenth position: hand on the soles of both feet.

The sole treatment is a summary treatment for the whole body. Having traveled all positions from the front, ask the person to turn their backs. And apply the healing energy in the positions described above.

Applying Reiki Energy in the positions described, we will have what is called complete Reiki.

This application, depending on the patient's need, should take from 20 to 40 minutes. This is the rule, but there are exceptions where the delay is longer.

We reinforce that these indications are only as a basis. By applying Reiki you may feel your hands "walking ". Let them go as it is your Reiki Guide directing you to where the application is needed.

It may also happen that the patient falls asleep. Don't wake him up abruptly. Just make a light, lightning-like touch on your arms and back. It is not necessary to call by name, but if the state of drowsiness persists, make movements in the arms and back calling it by name in a whispering voice.

When awake, start a conversation with the person. Ask how you felt, what you felt, if you dreamed, what you dreamed. Let her talk. It is at this time that we get rid of trauma experienced in another incarnation. Just listen with love and attention. Show interest, but don't guess. When he can "hear your Master" he will say what he must convey. In the meantime, just listen.

After the healing session, be sure to disconnect by washing your hands or just blowing them. This way you will not be overwhelmed with the patient's energy.

And finally, thank Father for having the opportunity to help a brother.

Channeling Reiki Energy Distance

The distant healing is one of the great benefits of healing by the Reiki energy. Using the Hon Sha Ze Sho Nen symbol enables us to send the healing energy at a distance connecting us with the Source of Everything. There are several ways to do distance healing.

When we do distance healing, time and distance cease to exist. Everything is just one thing.

Once the Source / healer / patient connection is made, energy begins to flow benefiting everyone involved in the process.

During a group healing session, the healer should use this symbol.

The aura, which is the field of human energy, is divided into sub-layers, each related to a specific function. They interpenetrate and surround each other in succession. These subdivisions of the aura are also called bodies. In distance healing the energy will act in the first three layers, as they are closer to the physical body.

Then we have the first layer, called the Etheric Body, which mediates energy and matter. It has the same shape as the physical body including all anatomical parts and organs. It would be like a mold where physical matter is fixed, a support for the physical body.

The second layer is the Emotional Body. It presents itself as colored clouds that have their hue associated with the feeling that the patient develops at that time.

The third layer is the Mental Body. It consists of substances associated with thoughts and mental processes. When we think we are moving energy that will influence our life. Manage the thoughts then, because it is through them that we will have positive or negative results.

This explanation was necessary for us to be aware that in distance Reiki, despite the speed with which it happens, the healing energy will primarily affect the mental and emotional bodies of the recipient. It will come to the physical by the ripple effect which will take a longer time for the physical pain to cease. But Reiki energy will always seek the cause, and heal it.

One way to channel Reiki healing energy is to arrange a time with the receiver to be receptive to the process of transmission. Beyond the schedule, we consider it vitally important that one mentions the Father in whatever way he conceives it. No matter the shape, the name. The important thing is that if we mentor Him, the promise of the Master Jesus will be fulfilled: where two or more people are speaking in My Name, I will be among them. What better company could we want...

We should not apply Reiki healing energy without the proper permission of the person not to injure free will. In the absence of such authorization, the Reiki Master should be requested from that person, and only after channeling.

Avoid sending Reiki to people who are working at risk or doing any activity that needs attention, as it may cause drowsiness.

Other Uses For Symbol

The use of symbols is unlimited.

Making a pass to remember:

Choku-Re - focuses on healing the physical body

Sei He Ki - Focuses on Healing the Emotional Body

Hon Sha Zé Sho Nen - Focuses on healing the mental body

Then use them simultaneously.

Whenever you draw or mentalize the symbol speak or mentalize your name three times.

Also use them to heal animals, plants, all living beings.

Use them also by aggregating to them the Seven Rays and transmute all negative energies of any material situation that presents itself.

Use them to put the energy needed to satisfy hunger in just one salad plate.

Use the symbols with discernment and responsibility, always respecting the free will of the people.

Desire Manifestation Technique

By working with symbols we can enjoy numerous benefits. This technique is one of them.

To use it, trace in the space below the three symbols mentalizing and pronouncing their names (mantras). Do the same on the last sheet of this book.

That done, write your requests and apply Reiki. Make a daily note of the request that was fulfilled, and apply Reiki again. Five minutes will be enough. If you have more requests, type.

Initiation as a Reiki healer is not an ending, but a starting point.

By allowing Reiki energy to enter our physical, mental and emotional bodies, we are giving us the opportunity to get rid of blockages, unwanted habits and physical ailments.

We make room for Source Energy to settle in, and the more space it fills in, the higher we will raise our level of consciousness.

And that's where the miracles will happen.

Who Can Benefit From REIKI?

Energy care is useful for all ages - for newborns and young children energy care allows them to calm, to calm down and connect to new energy exchanges with their parents after birth, for young children it allows them to channel their energies and concentration for adolescents and "adulescents" energy care allow them to pass a difficult course and to take root, to find their place and their way,

for adults young and old energy care allow them to open their chakras, to circulate the energies in their different bodies (physical, mental, emotional and spiritual) and harmonize.

For pregnant women (after 3 months), energy exchanges help strengthen the exchange parent / child best prepare the arrival e baby for older people, to help them endure: treatments, pain, pain, blockages....

Reiki offers energy treatments tailored to your needs at targeted treatments sessions, suitable for all audiences:

- For people before and / or after an operation or an accident to help scarring

- For people with reduced mobility or anyone with physical end-of-life disorders, to offer them a smooth accompaniment

153

- For people undergoing heavy care such as chemotherapy ...
- In the case of recurrent cancer-like diseases ...
- Aimed at relaxation, harmonization,
- Body / mind reconnection,
- "Healing" care (self-healing aid), self-recognition
- To determine blockages
- Treat anxieties, stress, malaise, depression ...

CONCLUSION

Thank you for making it through to the end of *Reiki Healing*, let's hope it was informative and able to provide you with all of the tools you need to achieve your goals whatever they may be.

As with everything, there are quality differences with Reiki. What to look for when choosing a competent Reiki teacher has been explained in this book. Also how to be attuned without being attuned or privy to Reiki experiences is in this book. Some of what you may have read in the book may sound "too good to be true.", but everything written about is an invitation to try it out. In life, only own authentic experiences count. Buddha said, "Do not believe anything just because the wise assert it. Do not believe, just because it has always been like that. Do not believe, just because others believe it. Test and experience everything yourself. "Reiki is not a belief system. If you are interested, you are welcome to be skeptical. This does not detract from the effect of Reiki.

Above all, Reiki is a self-help technique that we can use for others, even plants and animals. With Reiki, we make a valuable contribution to peace in this world, as we are constantly working intensely on our charisma, we increase the vibration on this planet and help the dark "cloud" of negative emotions, thoughts and actions that are still above the planet Earth lies to clear, to make our Earth a beautiful, bright blue planet again.

Chakra Healing

A Complete Meditation Guide on How the Chakras Work and How to Use Them to Improve Your Health and Awake the Positive and Vibrant Energy Within You With Yoga

Matthew Healing

Table of Contents

INTRODUCTION

Congratulations on purchasing *Chakra Healing*, and thank you for doing so.

The universe is full of energy, and it flows in, around, and through us. These energy flows impact how we feel, physically, emotionally, and spiritually. Blocked energy flows can lead to emotional, mental, and spiritual issues. They can even lead to physical illness.

These facts about the Universe that we live in have been known since ancient times, but as materialism rose to prominence in the west, this knowledge has been largely lost or abandoned in western cultures. That started to change in the 1960s when the preserved knowledge about energy and healing from India and other eastern cultures in Asia began to attract followers. Today, millions of people engage in yoga, meditation, and crystal healing and use tools from other Asian cultures such as acupuncture.

One thing all Asian cultures have in common is the recognition of Universal Energy and how it interacts with and influences the mind, spirit, and physical body.

In this book, we are going to introduce you to the seven major chakras. The chakras are energy centers in the body, and they have a profound influence on your wellness. In this introductory treatment, you will learn what the major energy centers in the

165

body are and how you can do your own energy healing through yoga and meditations. We will cover each of the seven major chakras in detail, learning the colors and elements associated with each one and learning the symptoms of blockages that can disrupt energy flow. These blockages can manifest in many ways on every plane of existence. This means that any given blockage can lead to physical, mental, emotional, or spiritual problems. We will learn what these problems are and how they manifest and give you simple exercises you can use to heal the energy flows in your body.

There are plenty of books on this subject on the market, so thanks again for choosing this one! Every effort was made to ensure it is full of as much useful information as possible. Please enjoy!

CHAPTER 1

THE SEVEN CHAKRAS

There are seven major chakras or energy centers in the body. They have a large influence on your well-being in the physical, mental, emotional, and spiritual planes. Having your chakras open and balanced is a key foundation for having a happy, healthy, and joyful life. In this chapter, we will introduce the seven major chakras and discuss the history of the chakras. The concept of energy interacting with the body is universal, but the concept of the chakras originated and was developed in India. Understanding the seven chakras also means understanding the symptoms of blockages, which disrupt energy flow through the body, and how to heal and unblock the chakras. We will be discussing the main techniques throughout the book.

What Are the Seven Chakras?

The seven major chakras are energy centers. They are located from the base of the spine to the top or crown of the head. Each chakra has an influence on different aspects of your life. Blockages or imbalances among the chakras can lead to problems in the physical, mental, emotional, and spiritual realms. As you study the seven major chakras, you will begin to realize where many problems in your life originate. Many people have blocked or unbalanced chakras. The nature and type of blockages are of significance, but the tools you need to open and heal the chakras lie within you and can even be done on your own in the privacy of your home.

When a chakra is blocked, this disrupts proper energy flow through the body. It is important to have each of the chakras fully open and in balance so that energy can flow the way it is meant to flow. If a chakra is out of balance, you will get too much of one aspect of your being expressed with the consequence that others are not fully expressed. We all know people who have suffered from sexual or gambling addictions or people who are so logical that they cannot recognize the spiritual or mystical side of existence. These are examples of people who have chakras that are out of balance and, therefore, expressing too much of one aspect of their nature at the expense of others.

One of the realizations one becomes aware of when studying eastern philosophy that is really rooted in common sense is that human beings (indeed, all beings to some degree) are equally rooted among different realities or aspects of being. For example, feeling pleasure is normal and a part of being human. But look at how many people around you (or maybe you, yourself) are suffering from an imbalance in this area, being obsessed with seeking pleasure? How many people have you known that let the pursuit of sexual pleasure, drinking, or gambling take over and, in some cases, destroy their lives? As we will come to understand in this book, these are examples of imbalances emphasizing the sacral chakra at the expense of others.

Common sense dictates that spiritual awareness and purpose is a higher part of the self. Indeed, this is true. And it is easy to see that a blockage of your higher self, in the form of empathy, spiritual purpose, and the like can lead to an obsession with the lower functions of the body that are geared toward physical pursuits.

But let's not get ahead of ourselves; we will learn about these things in detail as we proceed. For now, let's start getting acquainted with the seven major chakras. There are minor chakras as well, but it isn't required to know about them to heal the body and spirit; working with the major chakras is enough for most people. Of course, those who are interested in a more in-depth study are free to continue learning and study the minor chakras. But our focus in this book will be on the major chakras.

The seven major chakras, along with the physical location in the body, the color, and the Sanskrit name, are listed here. As we will see when meditating, knowing the color and physical location of the body is important. This is also important when doing yoga. The Sanskrit names are provided for reference so that if you are reading a text that uses the Sanskrit names, you will understand what they are talking about. We also provide these names for historical reference since the concept of the chakras and their study developed in ancient India.

The seven major chakras are:

- Root Chakra (Muladhara): Located at the base of the spine. The associated color is red.
- Sacral Chakra (Svadhishthana): Located on the front of the body just below the navel. The color is orange.
- Solar Plexus (Manipura): Located in the stomach area, below the rib cage but above the navel. The color is yellow.
- Heart Chakra (Anahata): Located in the center of the chest. The color is green.
- Throat Chakra (Vishuddha): Located at the base of the throat. The color is blue or turquoise.
- Third Eye (Ajna): Located just above the eyes in the center of the brow. The color is indigo.
- Crown Chakra (Sahasrara): Located on the crown of the head. The colors are purple, white, and gold.

Notice the progression of the colors, from red to blue to purple; this is no accident! The colors move through the colors of the rainbow. Scientists tell us that these colors correspond to the energy of light. Green light is more energetic than yellow or red light, for example. In the study of the chakras, higher energy vibrations correspond to more spiritual aspects of being. As we get into the details of each of the chakras, you will come to understand the energy associations and why each has higher energy and color than the previous chakra.

The locations in the body are not accidental, either. The closer you are to the earth, the more the physical aspects of being are emphasized. This is not to say that one is more important than the other in any fundamental sense. A truly spiritually awakened person has all aspects of their being awakened and in balance.

Although we describe the seven chakras as having physical locations, the energies associated with them are spiritual in nature. Therefore, it has a subtler quality, even though it is as real as anything in the universe if not more real.

Understanding the Chakra System

The word chakra comes from "wheel" and can be conceptualized as a spinning energy center. Chakras are in perpetual motion, drawing, and distributing energy. The energy drawn by the chakras comes from the universe itself and is all around you, transcending physical notions of space and time. Each energy wheel serves to drive different functions of the body and personality, including mind and spirit. Energy should flow upward through the spine, from Mother Earth to the crown chakra.

When a given chakra becomes blocked or is out of balance with the other chakras, problems can result. These can be multi-character; that is, a blocked chakra may impact your physical health, your emotional well-being, your mental states, or your spirituality. Or it may impact all of them simultaneously. As we will see, knowing the given symptoms that you are experiencing is a sign of what chakras you need to work on, using healing through meditation, yoga, and crystals. Affirmations can also help you balance and restore your chakras to health.

Many things can cause blockages of the chakras. Trauma or abuse from childhood, for example, can have lasting effects on the chakras. Recent events can also block chakras. The good news is that no matter the cause, there are standard and simple ways that can unblock chakras and promote healing.

Unlike western medicine, the eastern philosophies promote the whole being and recognize that we are spiritual and energy beings, not just physical beings. Of course, this does not mean that western medicine does not have its place. You can easily incorporate chakra healing with western medicine since the two work in completely different ways. In many cases, especially when mental and emotional issues are involved, chakra healing may be all that is needed.

The seven chakras can be visualized, as shown below:

Throughout the book, we will be covering each of the chakras in detail. However, here, we will provide a quick summary of what each chakra is associated with. This will help you begin to connect symptoms and imbalances in your life with each of the seven chakras.

Root Chakra

The root chakra is the lowest of the seven major chakras. But don't let this fool you; a person cannot try to elevate their spiritual being without having an open, healed, and balanced root chakra first. In fact, you should view all of the chakras in this way. That is, focus on healing each of the lower chakras in succession before you try opening or healing the higher, more spiritual chakras.

If you make the mistake of trying to open your third eye or crown chakra without having opened and balanced the lower chakras, it either won't work at all, or it could lead to serious problems of a spiritual and mental nature. Having a third eye awakening or attempting other spiritual paths, such as a kundalini awakening before you are fully developed, could lead to emotional trauma and unpleasant experiences.

As a beginner, it is important that you start with the fundamentals. This is similar to a medical doctor or any other expert. Would you want a doctor that skipped learning anatomy and just went straight to attempting brain surgery? Of course not. The same applies to your own spiritual development. You must establish a foundation for the body, mind, and spirit first. And that foundation begins with the root chakra.

The root chakra is most closely associated with Mother Earth, and it is related to our ability to be safe and secure in the physical world. A healed root chakra is associated with being able to meet our basic needs of shelter, food, and safety. The color is red because, relative to the other chakras, it is of lower energy in the spiritual sense. However, nothing in human experience can be separated from the spiritual side of life, and a blocked root chakra can induce many emotional and mental symptoms as a result.

Sacral Chakra

When you have your basic needs met, your attention turns to other physical needs and expressions. Naturally, sexuality and pleasure come to the surface when you have met your needs for food, shelter, and security. The sacral chakra is associated with the ability to feel pleasure and seeking it out. The sacral chakra is also associated with higher mental functions, in particular, creativity. Your creative juices flow from the sacral chakra. The color of the sacral chakra is orange, indicating higher energy than the root chakra.

An out-of-balance sacral chakra can be particularly dangerous. You might be correct if you imagine a blocked sacral chakra as manifesting as a lack of ability to feel pleasure, but many people go overboard with pleasure-seeking as a result of a lack in their being. On the other hand, if the sacral chakra is out of balance, then excessive devotion to pleasure can take place.

The type of pleasure associated with the sacral chakra is most closely associated with sexual and physical pleasure, but any kind of pleasure that a human being can experience is associated with the sacral chakra. So when you think of an out of balance or blocked sacral chakra, think of anything that may manifest here. It could be excessive alcohol consumption, drug use, or gambling. It could be excessive risk-taking in a supposedly "active" lifestyle, like rock climbing without using equipment or taking unnecessary risks for the sake of engaging in different activities. Anything that seems out of balance in regard to activities we derive pleasure from can be associated with the sacral chakra.

Solar Plexus Chakra

As we move up among the chakras, we see more spiritual aspects revealed. With the sacral chakra, it was creativity; with the solar plexus chakra, it is confidence, self-esteem, and self-assurance. It is often said that the solar plexus chakra is associated with confidence and a sense of purpose in the areas of work and career.

The color of the solar plexus chakra is yellow. Note that in order to have the solar plexus chakra open, balanced, and functioning properly, you must have an open and balanced root chakra, and you also need an open and balanced sacral chakra. You should work to heal your chakras in order: from the lowest to the highest. So if you were looking to heal your solar plexus chakra, you would begin working on the root chakra first, and then work on the sacral chakra when the root chakra had been opened, and then finally on the solar plexus chakra.

Heart Chakra

The heart chakra is at the center of the body's spirit. And this is not an accident. The root, sacral, and solar plexus chakras are considered to be "physical" chakras. This is not that they don't have an impact on your mind and spirit; they most definitely do because we are complete beings with aspects in all realities at all levels. That said, they tend to be more ego-based and have lower energy. They're more associated with childhood than with higher-level adult functioning. I tend to think of the root chakra as the chakra of childhood, while the sacral chakra begins to be expressed in early adolescence, and the solar plexus chakra takes shape in late adolescence and early adulthood (these are my own interpretations; not everyone will agree with them). This isn't to say that they are not important in adulthood; they are vital in adulthood, but like anything else, you grow with your foundations first, and this tends to happen in the earlier decades of life.

The heart chakra links together the higher and lower chakras. It serves as a linkage point between the lower, physical functions and the higher, more spiritual functions. We find that the heart chakra is associated with emotions like love and empathy, and the color is appropriately green. Caring about the other is an important aspect of the heart chakra, which reflects its higher value as compared to the lower chakras based more on ego and id.

176

Throat Chakra

Communication is an important aspect of interacting with others and getting our inner ideas out into the world. For this reason, it is a spiritual chakra, but like the heart chakra, it is still linked to the physical world. Once again, you should heal the lower chakras before attempting to heal the throat chakra, so if your solar plexus or heart chakra is out of balance, you should work on those before considering working on the throat chakra. The linkage between the throat chakra and the lower chakras is quite strong. Think about how the need to communicate truthfully and confidently is important in love relationships or in your career. This is an important observation, in my opinion, because it shows how the entire chakra system is integrated and cross-linked and how important it is to be balanced. The throat chakra represents the link between our inner mental and spiritual world and the outer physical world. It is associated with the colors blue and turquoise.

Third Eye Chakra

The third eye is the first purely spiritual chakra. It is associated with intuition and psychic abilities. You should not attempt to open the third eye before making sure all of the lower chakras are balanced. You might spontaneously experience an opening of the third eye; this could be indicated by lucid dreaming or knowing things that you should not know, including intuitive events about the future. The third eye is much higher energy, so it is associated with the color indigo or violet.

Crown Chakra

The crown chakra is located at the top of the head. This is the highest of the chakras, and it is related to our spirituality, our connection to the larger universe, the universal consciousness, and to other beings, including all life, living now, and those that lived in the past. The colors of the crown chakra are high energy, including purple, white, and gold. You connect with your Higher Self through the crown chakra.

How to Heal and Unblock the Chakras

These introductory discussions are very brief overviews. In the chapters that follow, we will dive deeply into each of the seven chakras and discuss symptoms that they are blocked or out of balance and how to heal them. We will discuss healing through meditation, mantras, affirmations, yoga, and using crystals.

It is important to realize that the chakras, while they have a significant impact on the physical body, exist in the spiritual plane. The colors that are associated with each chakra will help you attain the correct energy for each chakra during meditation, and this will help you heal and unblock the different chakras as necessary. We will also explore using colors in your environment to set the right energy for chakra healing and how you can use energy crystals of different colors to assist you in your spiritual work.

Meditation on a daily basis is the main tool that can be used to heal your chakras. We will discuss meditation in detail for each of the seven major chakras in the chapters that follow.

Yoga is also an optional but very useful tool that you can use to help heal and unblock your chakras and improve the energy flow throughout the body. In addition, you can consider the use of mantras and affirmations. You can combine affirmations with the appropriate crystal to help assist your efforts to unblock and heal your chakras. We will be giving you suggestions for these in the chapters that follow in each of the specific cases.

A Brief History of the Chakras

The concept of the chakras developed in ancient India, through a study of spirituality, meditation, and revelation of the truth. Knowledge of the chakras was first written down in a set of Indian spiritual texts called the Vedas. It is believed that the origin of the chakras (that is knowledge of and describing them) occurred sometime between 1500 and 500 BC, but the truth is that nobody knows. Evidence of knowledge of the meridians through tattoos has been found on Neolithic bodies that were preserved in the ice, so it's possible that knowledge of the chakras, meridians, meditation, and acupuncture goes well back into the stone age.

In any case, once a civilization had formed, the development of the chakra concept was found in India. They were mentioned in writing in the Upanishads around 750 BC. Locations and mantras associated with the chakras were noted in later Upanishads around 200 BC. They were discussed sporadically since, including in the 10th century. But it was during the 16th century that the chakra system was formally laid out by Swami Purananda. He wrote a book that included a chapter called the "Investigation of the Six Centers," which described the chakras, their functions, and how to activate them. He also discussed kundalini energy, a more advanced topic related to the chakras and spiritual awakening.

As Britain colonized India, the concepts of the chakras began to enter into western thinking. Translations of the book written by Swami Purananda were compiled in the early 20th century, opening up these ideas to people in English-speaking countries. As spiritual awareness outside of the usual confines of organized religion began to develop, including the influential visits by the rock band the Beatles, awareness of Indian spiritual practices became more widespread. Author and philosopher Christopher Hills wrote a book about the chakras in 1971, which opened up the idea of the association of colors to symbolize the energy of the seven chakras. The immigration of Yogi Bhajan to the United States at about the same time also increased western interest in these concepts.

CHAPTER 2

ROOT CHAKRA (MULADHARA)

The root chakra is the most fundamental of the chakras. It is located at the base of the spine and up through the first three vertebrae. The root chakra is the closest to Mother Earth and represents our basic grounding in life. Before you work on any of the other chakras, opening, healing, and balancing the root chakra is essential. Without its balance, we have no foundation in life. Think of it as a house; if you fail to build a solid foundation for a house, no matter how beautiful or well-constructed the rest of the house is, it cannot be truly stable and safe. Many people want to bypass the lower chakras and work right away on the spiritual chakras, but this is a mistake for the same reason. You might even have negative experiences if you work on your third eye and crown chakras without balancing the lower chakras first.

In contrast, if you build a solid foundation first, then you are creating the stability needed to build up your spirituality in a positive manner, leading to growth and harmony.

Color and Elements of the Root Chakra

The root chakra is denoted by the color red. This represents the lower energy of this chakra, which is not vibrating at the same high frequencies of the spiritual chakras, such as the third eye. Therefore, when you are working with the root chakra, you will want to surround yourself with the color red. This can be done in many different ways. For example, you can set aside a meditation room to use in the privacy of your own home and decorate it in red when you are working with the root chakra. This can be done with red pillows, drapes, and so on. In addition, you can use the appropriate crystals, and there are many that are red in color that can be utilized while working with the root chakra (however, not all crystals that are useful for this chakra are red in color). Ruby is an excellent example of a red crystal that you can use. You can also wear red-colored items of clothing when your focus is on the root chakra.

The element of the root chakra is earth. This is in the sense of Mother Earth, which provides all we need to be safe and nourished, including food, water, and shelter. The root chakra invokes the basic senses. The sense of smell is the most basic sense and most closely associated with the root chakra, but taste, sight, hearing, and touch are also associated with the root chakra. In addition, your "sense" of fear, safety is also connected to the root chakra.

The root chakra is represented by a red lotus flower with four lotus petals. The four petals represent the four parts of the human psyche. These are ego, intellect, mind, and consciousness.

Meaning of the Root Chakra

The first thing to think about with the root chakra is basic needs. We all have basic needs for food, shelter, safety, and security. In the modern world, this also includes financial security. Because the root chakra is closely associated with physical well-being, it is considered to be the first chakra of matter. The name of the root chakra in Sanskrit is *Muladhara*. The feelings associated with the root chakra are often thought of as instinctual. An animal also has needs for food, shelter, safety, and security. As such, the root chakra is often taken to be the chakra that manages our primal needs, including the fight-or-flight nature of our response to threats.

Of course, in the modern world, our bodies are put in situations where we react to non-primal situations and threats in a basic way because our cultural and scientific evolution has far outpaced our physical evolution. This means that in today's world, the root chakra is going to have an influence outside of purely physical needs. For example, you might have difficulties at work that can arouse a fight-or-flight response by the body. Of course, this is not accidental that this influences the root chakra because, in the modern world, there are many artificial means to survival that each of us must use. Although there was no money in our primal past, money is as real and essential for our survival, as staying out of the cold is. Indeed, it is money that determines whether we have a shelter or not.

The root chakra is also associated with a sense of belonging. This sense will exist on many different levels. For example, you will have a sense of belonging (or lack it) that is general in nature. Do you have a sense of belonging to Mother Earth, this place, and this time? If you do, then this is a sign that your root chakra is balanced. If you feel unease or a lack of belonging or that you don't fit in, then that can be a sign that you have a root chakra that is out of balance.

The root chakra is involved in all of our primal means of interacting with the world and obtaining information from it. This information is in the sense of "gut feelings," and the root chakra is closely tied to the five senses of taste, smell, touch, sight, and hearing. A newborn child interacts with the world primarily with the root chakra, and the other chakras only begin to develop as most of us get old. For this reason, early childhood experiences and trauma can have a large influence on the root chakra.

The trust in yourself and in others, especially closely related family members, comes from the root chakra. Being centered in your immediate family is the first form of security and safety that we feel. If this security is not provided, it can lead to long-lasting damage to the root chakra. Of course, you can overcome this damage, and in this series of books, we will be exploring the ways to do so.

So when you think of the root chakra, think of basic survival needs. Ask yourself questions about your survival needs. Do you feel safe at home? Do you feel safe while traveling? Do you feel like you are able to procure adequate food and other resources related to survival? Are you able to meet your financial obligations? Do you thoroughly trust those with whom you are having your closest and most significant relationships, including friends and family? These are all issues that are related to the root chakra. When your root chakra is in balance, you can say with confidence that you feel at home, whether that is in your actual physical home, in your job, with your family and friends, or anywhere.

Something to note about the root chakra is that it is based more on feelings than it is on logic. The root chakra is instinctual. Safety and security are going to be based more on feelings that they are thinking things through. When the root chakra is out of balance, it often acts as a feeding mechanism. There is no doubt that many readers have experienced this. That is, if your root chakra is out of balance and you are experiencing negative life situations related to security and financial stability, they seem to attract more insecurity and financial *instability*. Some people refer to this as the law of attraction. Since the nature of the root chakra is instinctual, it is the chakra that is the most prone to influence by the law of attraction (but of course, all the chakras are subject to this).

For this reason, meditation and mantras can be very effective when you are working to heal the root chakra.

When the root chakra is healed and balanced, you will feel safe and at home. You will feel comfortable around others and the choices you make. While you may not be "rich," you won't have any problems paying for your basic needs: food, shelter, transportation. You will feel perfectly safe and at home, and with friends and family members. Fear is not something that you will experience.

Emotional Signs of a Blocked Root Chakra

A blocked root chakra will create an imbalance of energy flow throughout the body, and due to its location at the base of the spine, you are likely to have problems with all the chakras if you are experiencing a blockage of the root chakra. A blockage may occur for many reasons. As we mentioned, childhood trauma is often a long-term cause of blocked root chakra. If you grew up with an unstable family life, this could also cause a blocked root chakra. Trauma in adulthood can also cause blockages, even normal events that take place in the course of one's life. For example, the sudden death of a parent, even when you are an adult, can lead to the root chakra being blocked. This is because the world of stability that you have known all of your life is suddenly disrupted. If your root chakra is already out of balance, experiences such as these can lead to destabilizing results.

If you have a blocked root chakra, you are going to be prone to worry and anxiety. You might feel restless, and since the root chakra is associated with security at home and feeling at home, a blocked root chakra can lead one to feel restless and unable to "settle down." People often take action in life, and they aren't sure why. One way this manifests with the root chakra is that you might move around a lot. You will rent rather than buy a home. You might avoid solid connections in relationships because you are unable to "settle down." You can be unsure of where you want to work, or even what career you want to pursue. Did you have trouble picking a major in college? Someone who never feels satisfied, drifting from major to major, might have a blocked root chakra.

A person with a blocked root chakra is always searching, and yet never finding what they are looking for. Satisfaction in life seems ever elusive. A feeling of abandonment may be pervasive, leading one to avoid forming long-lasting ties in relationships because doing so seems futile, and the person with a blocked root chakra would prefer the safety of being alone to the risk of being emotionally hurt.

A lack of focus is common among those with a blocked root chakra, and that is why problems like being unable to settle on a major in college are common. Anxiety disorders are common, and obsessive-compulsive disorder can often be traced to the root chakra being blocked.

Among the most common mental and emotional signs of a blocked root chakra are the following:

- A lack of focus
- Constant worry and anxiety
- Feeling unsafe at home
- Feeling unsettled and constantly unsure about choices made in life
- An inability to form long-lasting, close relationships
- Not able to make commitments. This is a general problem, not limited to relationships but also to jobs and a course of study
- Constantly moving from place to place, unable to settle
- Unable to hold a job
- Having financial problems. When it comes to having blocked root chakra, these will be of the most fundamental nature. So while some people might have financial problems related to paying taxes or large debts, someone with a blocked root chakra will have financial problems related to meeting the basic needs. This means they will be unable to pay rent in a timely manner, as well as utilities. They are not secure when it comes to buying food. A person with a blocked root chakra will, for some reason, never have enough money, even though they are not leading a lavish lifestyle.
- Feelings of abandonment. They can be vague or specific.
- Prone to panic attacks
- Unable to trust others

- Feelings of frustration that can result from never being able to achieve goals
- Anger and rage that flow from the feelings of frustration
- Feelings of guilt or resentment

Physical Symptoms of Blocked Root Charka

If you have a blocked root chakra, it may manifest in physical, as well as mental and emotional symptoms. Often, the physical symptoms that manifest can be a result of generalized anxiety and constant worry, so it won't surprise you that one physical symptom that people often experience is high blood pressure. Other symptoms, like impotence, are an indirect result of feelings of anxiety, guilt, and resentment.

Other physical symptoms are focused on the lower part of the body, such as sciatica or foot pain. We can summarize the physical symptoms of a root chakra blockage as follows:

- Digestive problems: These often result from the anxiety associated with the root chakra being blocked. They can manifest as constipation, diarrhea, or irritable bowel syndrome.
- Hypertension: High blood pressure can result from a constant state of mind where you experience anxiety, worry, and feeling unsafe. These emotional states raise the level of stress hormones, like cortisol, in the body, and this can contribute to a feeling of "tension" that has real physical effects, such as high blood pressure. Of course, this is a serious medical problem. Try to see if you can

reduce your blood pressure through meditation, yoga, and healing of the root chakra. If not, then you will need to discuss the proper medications with a western medical doctor.

- Sciatica: Lower back and leg pain can result from a blocked root chakra. Yoga can help with this.
- Prostate problems
- Eating disorders

Financial Problems, Focus, and Goals

In the modern world, our basic needs for survival are met through the use of money and work. So I am pulling out this topic for special mention here because a blocked root chakra will often manifest very strongly in the areas of work and money, and this can include the ability to focus and meet goals. If you are having problems focusing and meeting goals, this is a strong indication that you have a blocked root chakra. You can see this manifest in a myriad of ways. For example, you might have trouble holding a job for a significant time period. This can impact you in other ways, indirectly. People who cannot hold jobs often fail to get ahead financially because career advancement is an important aspect of increasing your income.

A person with a blocked root chakra will be in one of two states. They are often a "drifter," moving from job to job, often not having a job, and this can also include moving from place to place. Or you might find that you are chronically "underemployed." Despite having skills and credentials, you feel "trapped" in a job that is not utilizing your skills or paying you what you are really worth in the marketplace. When in these types of situations, one of the most telling symptoms of a blocked root chakra is a tendency to blame the outside world for such problems. People with a blocked root chakra who have a low-paying job that is below their real qualifications will blame their boss, the company, or the world in general. You will see the same type of mindset among those who are constantly moving from job to job. They will blame the outside world for their circumstances.

In other words, one of the symptoms of a blocked root chakra that is often overlooked is an attitude that everything that happens to you is somebody else's fault. If you feel that you may have a blocked root chakra, you should take a look at your mindset and see if this describes your situation. One way to combat this is to use daily affirmations that will emphasize your role in being responsible for your own outcomes.

You may also have trouble setting goals and reaching them. This can occur in several different ways. Of course, the first way that this can happen is not setting goals at all. Someone who constantly blames others for their problems is probably not going to be setting goals to improve their life situation. Another way that this can manifest is when you set goals that are not really attainable. In this case, goals are nothing more than fantasy since each goal that is set is so outlandish; it is not possible to move from your present situation in order to attain the goal (such as "I want a million dollars"). Others will have vague notions of goals, but they are unable to plan or execute them. Being unable to plan and execute is another symptom of a blocked root chakra.

191

In the end, having enough money to live in a secure home where you feel safe is going to be the first sign of a healed root chakra. It doesn't matter if the home is large or small, if it is a house or apartment, or if it is urban or rural. The thing that matters here is that it is a safe place where you truly feel at home. If you do not feel secure in your present home, you might ask yourself if this is due to a blocked root chakra, and if so, how this is manifesting. That is, it could be manifesting in the choices you make. People with a blocked root chakra may subconsciously choose to live in insecure situations, and then after they are in the situation, they start looking to the external world for the reasons. That is, if they even think about that at all, many will simply accept the feelings of insecurity and believe that this is just "the way it is." In many cases, the home can be made safe and secure, but a blocked root chakra is getting in the way. You can use meditation and crystals to deal with this type of situation.

You don't want to overanalyze your situation; you should look toward using meditation and other techniques so that the answer will come to you. Then you will know what actions to take. It is important not to give in to the urge to simply move to another location unless an objective view is that the home you live in is really not a safe place.

In addition to feeling secure in the home, look to see how your finances are impacting your ability to pay your basic bills. The basic bills do not include things like student loans, credit card debts, and so forth, although managing debt is something that can be related to the root chakra. By basic bills, we mean items related to survival:

- Paying your water bill
- Having enough money to buy food without any outside assistance
- Keeping the electricity and gas on
- Paying a phone bill for communication

People with a blocked root chakra are often chronically late when paying for their utilities and even have them shut off periodically. The inability to pay for basic needs often underlies problems, stemming from a blocked root chakra. These can be related to being underemployed or having trouble holding jobs. The person may also hold a job but may be unable to control their spending in other areas, so they rack up credit card debts or spend outside their means, leaving them unable to meet the basic needs. If you find yourself in these kinds of situations, or you possibly don't have enough to eat because you are driving an expensive car or spending wildly on credit, then you might be lacking the grounding that a balanced root chakra provides.

I have singled out financial issues in this chapter because this is often one of the most fundamental ways that a blocked root chakra will manifest, along with general feelings of insecurity. If you have these kinds of issues, of course, there is worthwhile advice from financial experts and coaches on how to fix your financial issues. But the real issue is a blocked root chakra. So you need to fix that first; otherwise, attempts to fix financial issues are probably going to leave you going around in circles.

Spiritual Problems

The root chakra is a chakra of "matter" or a physical chakra. That said, if you do not feel safe and grounded in your ability to satisfy your basic, most fundamental needs of survival, there really isn't time or energy to deal with spirituality. One of the symptoms of a blocked root chakra is that spiritual concerns are pushed to the "backburner" if they are considered at all. When you have a blocked root chakra, feelings of insecurity may keep you from devoting any attention to your spiritual needs.

You may find yourself in a situation where you cannot even think of them at all. Instead, your mind is consumed with constant worry and anxiety, often about getting through each week and the commitments required. Alternatively, people will devote their spiritual attention to ask for safety and security rather than spiritual growth. If you find that either you are not thinking about your Higher Self or any of your spiritual needs at all, or you notice that you are constantly praying for safety and security, or for money to appear to pay a bill, these can indicate that you have a blocked root chakra.

Healing a Blocked Root Chakra With Meditation

A blocked root chakra can be healed using a combination of meditation, mantras, daily affirmations, and yoga. You can also work on your root chakra by emphasizing and surrounding yourself with red colors and using crystals. However, meditation is the fundamental and core activity that should be used to heal the root chakra or any of the chakras. In this section, let's set up the basic meditation that can be used. Meditation goes a long way toward healing the root chakra if practiced daily. For one, it will promote relaxation and reduce anxiety and worry besides helping you to direct the right frequency of energy to the right locations in your body.

The first step that is necessary for the successful use of meditation is to have a quiet space that is used for this purpose. Your space should be a location where you will not be disturbed for at least 15 minutes at a time. I also recommend that you meditate completely alone. Meditation is for you and your energy, and it is important that you are able to look inward and completely focus, so it should be a location that is quiet and safe and a place where you can be alone for "me time."

Second, your meditation space should be one that is flexible so that it can be decorated in different colors. This helps to set the overall energy of the space and, therefore, for your meditation. For the root chakra, you want to primarily use the color red for the meditation space. So if you can decorate the room with red pillows, drapes, and so forth, this will help to make the meditation more effective.

You can also enhance this effect by wearing red clothing during your meditation on the root chakra.

Begin by assuming the easy pose position. Sit on the floor with your legs crossed in front of you, back straight. Place your hands about where your knees are, palms up, and touch the thumb to the index finger to close the energy circle, and close your eyes. If you have problems sitting in this position, you can sit on a pillow, and, if necessary, place your back against a wall or other object that can provide support. The easy pose is illustrated below.

Close your eyes, and breathe rhythmically and deeply. Each meditation session should last 15 minutes at a minimum, up to 30 minutes, depending on your time commitment. At a minimum, you should meditate each morning, but if you can also meditate in the evening, this can be helpful.

Remember that you need to heal the root chakra before attempting to work on any of the higher chakras. You should heal your chakras in order, so do not move from the root chakra because you are anxious to make progress. Move to the next chakra when you feel you have truly made progress in healing and opening the root chakra.

You can say a mantra during your meditation to assist your spiritual development. For beginners, simply say LAM. This is a simple mantra that can be used to heal the root chakra.

There are many kundalini mantras that can be used to enhance your meditations, but as a beginner, you should avoid these. A beginner is not someone who wants to attempt to awaken kundalini energy, so please focus on using the LAM mantra until you have healed all seven major chakras. You can say LAM loudly or inside your mind, but it's not necessary, in my opinion, to say it at all; you can do what you are comfortable with.

Visualization is a very important part of the meditation process. Therefore, you should be working on visualizing the color red. The way that we visualize in meditation for the chakras can take one of two forms. The first is that you can visualize a spinning circle of energy. Remember that the term "chakra" is related to the concept of a spinning wheel. Using your mind's eye is key to the visualization, so you are going to want to close your eyes for the length of the meditation. Visualize a deep black background so that the colors can take on a central aspect of your vision. Against the black background, see a bright, spinning red disk of light. I try to see it with a bright, fluorescent quality. See this light emerging from the earth below you, spinning slowly at first. The goal is to see the ball of light, gaining energy slowly as it moves up through your body to the point where the chakra is located.

You can also use four lotus leaves as your visualization. The example is below that can serve to guide you. You can find more examples if you search for them.

The details are not as important as making sure that you focus on the color red.

See the spinning wheel entering your body from below and slowly moving upward to the root chakra at the base of your spine. As it moves upward, see the spinning disk begin to spin faster. Your entire focus should be on the disk of light and any mantras that you are saying. Learning to focus in this fashion will help to heal the root chakra in addition to aiding your later meditations. If you are completely new to meditation, don't worry if you are having a hard time concentrating, that is a normal part of development. You may wish to start with shorter meditation sessions and work up to fifteen minutes if you have trouble staying focused in the beginning.

A second method of meditating that has been proposed is to visualize a spinning ball of red light in front of you. Breathe deeply and methodically. With each breath, take in some of the red light. As time progresses, imagine the light growing brighter and more powerful. As you near the end of the meditation session, imagine your body becoming completely enveloped in bright red light, and see this red light filling every aspect of your being.

One method that has been proposed for meditation with regard to the root chakra is to meditate while saying the affirmation, "I am safe and secure. I am stable and grounded." To do this meditation, say the affirmation after you breathe out. So sit quietly with your eyes closed, visualizing a spinning ball of red light before you. Then breathe in deeply, hold the breath for a moment, and breathe out and say the affirmation. Repeat this for a period of 15 minutes.

A *mul* mantra meditation can also be very productive with the root chakra. The *mul* mantra, in English, is said as follows:

One Creator. Truth is His name. Doer of everything. Fearless, Revengeless, Undying, Unborn, Self-illumined, The Guru's gift, Meditate! True in the beginning. True through all the ages. True even now. Oh, Nanak, it is forever true.

This is a kundalini mantra, so it should be used after you have healed the seven chakras, and you are ready to elevate your efforts and pursue a kundalini awakening. This mantra will help you build a solid spiritual foundation, so this can be seen as a way to meditate on the root chakra from a higher perspective, rather than simply concerning your physical safety and security. Meditate for several minutes while saying the mantra.

Finally, another method that has been proposed for root chakra meditation is to learn how to focus. For beginners, properly focusing during meditation is one of the most difficult things to learn. Therefore, this can be particularly important.

This method can be used for any chakra. In the case of the root chakra, I propose using an artificial light source that emits the color red. You might investigate using a mobile application that is built for this purpose. It can help to be in a dark room so that the red color of the light from your device becomes prominent. Then meditate with the sole purpose of focusing on your breath. That is, breathe in and out slowly and deeply, and focus your entire attention on the breath. Don't worry if this is not easy to do in the beginning. As a beginner, you might have thoughts intruding on the experience, or you have your attention distracted by any number of things. Keep practicing, and over time, you will get better.

Music and Other Aids to Use While Meditating

You can find relaxing eastern music (in particular from India, or singing bowls, but any eastern themed music will do as long as it is relaxing in nature) to use with your meditation. Some people find that it helps to have this type of music playing in the background while they are meditating, while others prefer complete quiet. The goal is to let go of the self and focus on the light during the meditation, so you should do what works best for you.

Guided Meditations

There are also many guided meditations that can be used. You can find these online, and there are many high-quality, free meditations on YouTube. These meditations are good to use for beginners because they can help you learn what you should visualize. In addition, you can become familiar with the sounds or music that should be used during meditation, along with mantras. If you use guided meditations, I recommend using two meditation sessions per day, and you can use one session with a guided meditation and one session that is not guided. There are also many apps available on the different app stores that can help you with guided meditations or simply with visualizing the colors. However, it is not generally recommended that you work too much with electronic devices, and I prefer to have the meditation room free of too many electronic devices other than lighting and playing background music. This is especially important when it comes to using a phone; the last thing you want is to have your meditation interrupted by phone calls and text messages. So, shut your phone off and leave it in another room during your meditation sessions. If you decide to use apps for guided meditations, use the apps as an adjunct to your main meditation. Remember to stay focused, so if you are working on the root chakra, use your apps to heal the root chakra. Don't give in to the temptation to move on to other chakras until you are ready to do so.

There are many guided meditations for the root chakra on internet that you can use for free.

Singing Bowls

Although it is from a different spiritual tradition, Tibetan singing bowls can be very useful during meditation for background music. You can get recordings of Tibetan singing bowls and also find apps and free examples on YouTube to use. You can even get your own singing bowl and then use them to help establish a relaxed state of mind before meditation. This is very effective.

Affirmations for the Root Chakra

One of the best ways to heal your chakras is to use the appropriate daily affirmations to heal problems that arise from being out of balance or having a blocked chakra. Pick the affirmations that are the most relevant to your situation and say them three to five times, in two to three sessions per day. Our minds are guided in part by subconscious programming that we received over the years, often going back deep into childhood.

Here are some suggestions to get you started. These affirmations are designed to help heal the root chakra.

- I feel safe and secure.
- I am able to meet my needs.
- I can earn enough money to pay my bills.

- I spend my money wisely.
- I am comfortable with who I am.
- I know what I want and how to get it.
- I feel safe at home.
- My house is truly a home that is welcoming and safe.
- My root chakra is fully open and balanced.
- I feel calm and relaxed.
- I deserve financial security.
- I feel safe and protected.
- Mother earth gives me all that I need.
- With every breath, I release worry and anxiety.
- I am in control of my future.
- I am in control of my finances.
- I have the power to change my life.
- I have the power to be safe.
- I am becoming successful.
- I have the power to earn as much money as I need.
- I can choose where to live.
- I never have problems paying my bills.
- I am free from limiting thoughts.
- I can do anything I set my mind to.
- I am free from fear.
- I have a purpose in life.
- I am attracting wealth and abundance.
- I will allow myself to feel grounded.
- I will allow myself to feel safe.
- I accept the protection of Mother Earth.
- I feel connected to friends and family and can count on others for support.

Use affirmations in the morning and in the evening to help you create the right mindset that goes along with an open and healed root chakra. You can say the affirmations whenever you need them and feel free to create your own affirmations for the root chakra.

Five Yoga Poses for the Root Chakra

Although it is not strictly required, doing yoga can be a great way to open and heal your chakras, and it can be an important part of your overall spiritual journey. In this section, we are going to briefly go over five yoga poses that are particularly useful for the root chakra. Yoga is particularly good for healing the physical symptoms that are associated with each chakra, but they also assist in healing the mental, emotional, and spiritual symptoms associated with blockages by helping to open the channels necessary for proper energy flow.

One of the goals of yoga poses for the root chakra will be to enhance lower body strength. This is important because we want to feel strongly rooted in Mother Earth in order to have an open and balanced root chakra. In addition, you will want to open up the lower spinal area that will help with energy flow.

When doing yoga, you will want to breathe deeply and slowly. Start by holding each pose for a minimum of 10-12 breaths. As you gain strength and get more comfortable doing yoga, you can work your way up to holding your pose for 30 breaths or so, or up to three minutes. If you don't feel comfortable in the beginning, just hold the pose for 10 breaths, and you can increase the length of time in each pose as you gain strength and flexibility.

Sukhasana

This is the easy pose we suggest using for meditation. This easy pose will assist in opening the root chakra because it will stretch out and lengthen the spine, helping to open the root chakra. The position will also help you by opening up the hip area, making your body more receptive to energy.

Description

You can either sit on the floor or on a pillow, or folded towels or blankets that are 4-6 inches in thickness. Sit with back straight and cross your legs in front of you, so that one shin is on top of the other, placing each foot beneath the opposite shin. Let your feet relax, and place your hands on top of your knees, palms upward. You can touch the second finger of each hand to the thumb, if desired to form a connection. Alternatively, you can place your hands in the prayer position.

Malasana

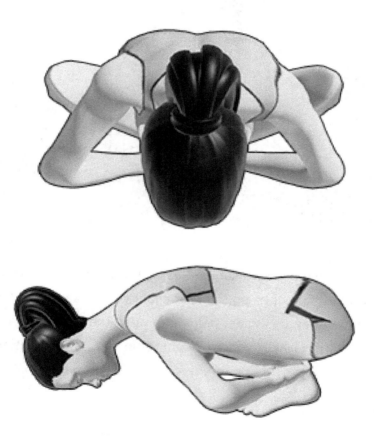

This is actually a set of poses that involve squatting. I will suggest this as an optional pose for beginners because it can be a more difficult pose that is hard on the knees for some people. If you are a beginner, you can start using it for short periods and increase its use with time. The basics of the pose are to have the feet close together and the back in a rounded position, which opens up the spine and, hence, opens up the root chakra.

You can actually start working up to this pose from the easy pose. As a beginner in yoga, if you have no experience, try sitting in the easy pose first and simply bend forward, moving your face to the floor to open up the spine area. In fact, that method will work for many, but you can move to the full malasana pose with time so that you can start building lower body strength. Lower body strength is actually an important component of the root chakra and root chakra healing.

Description

Begin in the Sukhasana position. Then lift yourself up on your feet, to raise your body 4-6 inches. Now lean forward to curve the back of the spine, until you are face down on the floor. Hold the position for about one minute.

Bridge pose

The bridge pose is another exercise that will help strengthen the lower back and the muscles of the buttocks and hamstrings. Begin by laying on your back, and then lift up the pelvic region to assume a pose as shown below:

Grasp your hands behind your back, as shown in the image. For many, this is going to be a difficult pose to maintain, so start slowly to avoid injury, but you will find this pose effective, both for opening up the spine and for building lower body strength.

Description

Lay down flat on the floor. Lift your legs straight up and bend your knees, with your feet placed flat on the floor. The feet should be close together, but spread apart at the width of your hip bones. Push your tailbone upward, and then clasp your hands together underneath your body, positioned approximately below the buttocks area.

Urdhva Mukha Svanasana

This is a back-bending asana that, in English, is known as the facing dog pose. This will help to strengthen the lower back and abdominal muscles while also serving to open up the lower energy centers of the body.

Description

Begin this pose laying face down on the floor, as if you were going to do a pushup. Your legs should be stretched out straight behind you. Now push straight up. Arch the back upwards to curve it, and turn your head backwards, so that your face is angled toward the ceiling.

Virabhadrasana (Warrior II)

The Warrior II pose will help open up the body and the root chakra. This is a standing pose that is taken in the following position:

The warrior II pose will also serve to strengthen the thigh muscles.

Description

Start standing straight, and then turn the right side of your body fully to the right. Lean down with your right knee. Your right food should be at a 90 degree angle, so facing to the right. Your left foot should still be facing straight forward. Lift both arms up and stretch them both out from the body, with palms flat, facing downward. The right hand should be aligned in direction with the right foot, and the left hand should be exactly 180 degrees from the right hand, pointing straight away from the left shoulder. Turn your face in the direction of the right hand. Repeat the pose in the other direction with left and right reversed.

In addition to yoga, you can do any exercises that will stretch and open up the back, as well as any exercises that will strengthen the lower parts of the body. Focus on strengthening the hamstrings, thigh muscles, and lower abdominal muscles. You can also work on strengthening the calf muscles. Any exercises that help you feel more "rooted" and strong, as well as connected to the earth, will help to heal and open the root chakra. The exercises described here can be a permanent part of your routine to help keep your root chakra open and balanced. In the beginning, you will want to focus on them before moving on to the other chakras.

Crystals for the Root Chakra

Several crystals can be used to help heal the root chakra and your living space. Black tourmaline is a good crystal to use for this purpose. It can be placed at all four corners of a room in order to help make it a secure living space. You can also put this in your car to enhance safety and security while traveling. Any "grounding" stone is suitable for working with the root chakra. This includes bloodstone. Both bloodstone and black tourmaline are inexpensive. Ruby is also an excellent stone to use when healing the root chakra. You can hold any of these stones during meditation, and wear them on your body as needed.

CHAPTER 3

THE SACRAL CHAKRA

The next chakra that is above the root chakra is the sacral chakra. In this chapter, we will talk about problems that can arise when your sacral chakra is blocked or out of balance. The sacral chakra is still a chakra of matter or a physically oriented chakra, but the impact of the sacral chakra will reverberate throughout your entire being, including the physical, mental, emotional, and spiritual aspects. Also, as we move up the chakras, we incorporate more of the mental aspects of our lives, slowly moving up our needs based on Maslow's hierarchy of needs. It is interesting to note that as you move up the chakras, you also encounter not only more mental, emotional, and spiritual components but also an increasing level of maturity. For an analogy, you can think about how you develop your ego before being able to feel empathy for others or think outside of the perspective of your infantile self that needs to have her basic needs satisfied.

The sacral chakra is primarily associated with sexuality and reproduction, and the ability to feel or experience pleasure. But, reflecting the fact that this is a higher level chakra than the root chakra, we also find creativity and the expression of creativity associated with this chakra. We also note that this chakra vibrates at a higher frequency than the root chakra.

The Sanskrit name for the sacral chakra is *Swadhisthana*.

Color and Elements of the Sacral Chakra

The colors of the rainbow move from lower energy light that is red in color into higher energy light that progresses from orange to yellow, green, blue, indigo, and violet or purple. Likewise, it is the same as the energies of the chakras. The sacral chakra is higher than the root chakra and is, therefore, represented by a color of higher vibrational frequency, which, in this case, is orange. The orange color of the sacral chakra nicely captures its sexual and creative components. Orange is a color, especially when considering bright orange, which captures the emotional essence and energy of sensuality on an intuitive level. Orange represents fiery energy but in a controlled sense.

The element most closely associated with the sacral chakra is water. This choice is appropriate because the sacral chakra is associated with flow and flexible movement of energy. The sacral chakra is also associated by some with the lymphatic system of the body, so it can play a role in generalized health, and you can see how the flow is an important aspect of this.

When represented by the lotus flower, the sacral chakra has six petals (remember, the root chakra has four petals). The sound for the sacral chakra is VAM.

Meaning of the Sacral Chakra

A healthy and balanced sacral chakra is necessary for a person to be able to enjoy life to the fullest. Although many people associate the sacral chakra solely with sexual energy, the truth is the sacral chakra is more general than that; it is actually associated with the general ability to feel and experience pleasure of all kinds. That does not minimize the sexual association with this chakra; sexual pleasure and reproduction are definitely associated with the sacral chakra. If you are attempting to determine if the sacral chakra is blocked, you will want to think in terms of general enjoyment, although sexual issues are often a symptom of a blocked sacral chakra.

Also, we will restate the advice we have given earlier, which is actually quite essential. That is, you need to have your chakras unblocked, balanced, and healed in order from low to high. A blocked root chakra may put you in a position where you think you have a blocked sacral chakra. But try and imagine having a blocked root chakra and the fact that if you are feeling aimless, full of anxiety, and lacking any feelings of safety and security. You are going to have problems with sexuality and enjoying any pleasure as well. If you heal the root chakra, it may eliminate many of those problems without having to put a great effort into healing the sacral chakra.

The sacral chakra is also associated with gut-level intuition, although when we think of intuition, it is mostly the third eye that is of importance here.

When the sacral chakra is open and balanced, you are able to express your sexual energy and enjoy pleasures of all types without fear or guilt. You will also be able to do so in a balanced fashion. A healthy person is able to enjoy their sexuality without becoming obsessed with it, and this is a key fact to keep in mind when evaluating the health of your own sacral chakra. Does your life feel in complete balance and harmony?

It's also important not to get too tied up in the association with pleasure that the sacral chakra is known for. The role that the sacral chakra plays in creativity is important for you to consider so that you can unleash your full sense of being. When you let your creative juices flow, this will help in all aspects of your life, including at work and in interpersonal relationships. This brings us back to the fact that the element of the sacral chakra is water because creativity thrives when your psychic and emotional energy is able to flow unimpeded. Flexibility is also something that is closely associated with creativity.

The sacral chakra awakens all of the five physical senses and integrates them with our conscious mind. This is important in order to be able to experience the pleasures that life has to offer to the fullest extent possible. Therefore, like the root chakra, you can think of the sacral chakra as integrating with all five of the physical senses, beginning with the sense of touch, which is fundamental. It is also closely tied with sight, sound, taste, and smell. The ability to enjoy any sensation, whether it's the pleasant smell of a flower, the taste of a good meal, or the feeling of being touched romantically, all stem from the sacral chakra. The more you open the sacral chakra, the more you will feel the world that we live in. An open and balanced sacral chakra enables you to feel every sensation, taste, or smell with the utmost intensity, while a blocked sacral chakra can leave you feeling that the world is dull, boring, and empty.

The sacral chakra is also tied with many of our emotions, and these emotions are more primitive and ego-based in nature, yet they are essential to our status as complete beings. That said, as you know from your own experiences, the impact that the sacral chakra has on our primitive emotional states can reverberate throughout our entire being. This is why so many people have such dramatic problems with many aspects of pleasure, whether it's through addiction or the seemingly inevitable conflicts that can arise throughout the course of life and our interactions with others. In fact, when the sacral chakra becomes blocked, the emotional states that can result can even become all-encompassing, even destroying a person's life. If the balance is important for any of the chakras, it is central to the sacral chakra.

Let's summarize the meaning of the sacral chakra with a few key points and concepts:

- The sacral chakra is closely associated with your ability to sense, feel, and enjoy pleasure and sensuality.
- The primary type of pleasure that is often associated with the sacral chakra is sexual pleasure. However, all types of pleasure and your ability to experience them flow through the sacral chakra. This can include anything that can be associated with pleasure: from enjoying a hobby to a good meal or sensual touch.
- A balanced sacral chakra enables you to experience and to express your sexuality freely in a healthy way. You can do so without guilt, exploiting others, or becoming obsessed.
- A healthy sacral chakra will help your relationships.
- The sacral chakra helps keep the "raw" primitive emotions associated with sexuality in a healthy and balanced state.
- The sacral chakra is involved with creativity, and, in particular, with helping creative energy flow freely and without constraint.
- Fantasies, whether they are sexual in nature or imaginative and creative, are associated with the sacral chakra.
- Those with a healthy sacral chakra are able to enjoy all physical pleasures to the fullest and freely experience the physical world that we live in. When in balance with all of the other chakras, this is done without being overwhelmed by pleasure.

- A healthy sacral chakra helps you to be flexible and assists you in getting along with others.

Emotional and Mental Issues Associated With a Blocked Sacral Chakra

A blocked sacral chakra is a very dangerous type of blockage indeed. In fact, many people will end up destroying their lives over a blocked sacral chakra. It can lead to unhealthy obsessions with sex and other addictions, and it can act to create drama and other problems in relationships. It leads a person to feel dominated by primitive emotions while ignoring their Higher Self and the spiritual aspects of their existence and the world that surrounds them.

The way that a blocked or out of balance sacral chakra manifests may vary from person to person. One of the key ways that it can manifest is feeling dead to the world. If your sacral chakra is blocked, often, you will be unable to feel pleasure at all. Interestingly, even here, we see a huge variation in how a person can react to this situation. In some cases, a blocked sacral chakra that leads to a person feeling dead to pleasure leads them to completely withdraw. This is the expected course of action. For example, if you cannot feel sexual pleasure, you will avoid sexual activity. If you are married or in a relationship, you will avoid physical contact with your partner.

A lack of sexual desire is very common among those who have a blocked sacral chakra. This can also express itself in other ways. The inability to feel pleasure may go well beyond the sexual realm, and it can impact a person's ability to enjoy anything involving physical pleasure. This can lead a person to overemphasize other aspects of their life in order to compensate. For example, they may become too involved in their work life. Or they can become obsessed with any activities that minimize the role of sexuality in their lives. For example, many people become highly active in charities related to animal welfare, the elderly, or other activities. Don't misunderstand. Getting involved in those types of charities is certainly desirable and good! We are simply pointing out that *some* people will get involved in these kinds of activities that go *beyond the self* as a result of a blocked sacral chakra, doing so in a manner that is unhealthy and unbalanced so that they can compensate for the lack of pleasure that they are able to feel like a part of the sexual and sensual aspects of their being. In other words, a healthy human being is one who is completely balanced and is, therefore, able to enjoy physical pleasure, value the self, and go beyond the self as an additional aspect of their life, not to replace certain aspects of their being.

Many people with a blocked sacral chakra feel numb, and this is a general feeling that is expressed in every aspect of their lives. They eat because they have to, but they lack the normal enthusiasm that people feel for a good meal. They don't enjoy waking up in the morning, and they work only because they have to. They will lack any passions in life, whether it's in the form of hobbies, their career, or other activities or causes.

Feeling out of touch with yourself and as though you are leading a life that is without purpose are also symptoms that may indicate a blocked sacral chakra.

Interestingly, however, the sacral chakra can manifest in the completely opposite manner when it is not healthy. That is, people become obsessed with pleasure-seeking and exhibit many addictive behaviors.

Sexual addiction is an obvious sign of a blocked or out of balance sacral chakra. This is a pretty interesting phenomenon, in that the same blocked sacral chakra might lead one person to feel completely numb and lead to a withdrawal from sexual activity because of a complete lack of desire, while another person may become overwhelmed with sexual desire, to the point that it is destructive in their overall life.

Sexual addiction isn't the only way that this can manifest. Addiction to any substance, whether it's alcohol, cigarettes, or drugs, is another way that a blocked sacral chakra can manifest. Gambling addiction can also occur. And of course, you often find all these addictions expressed in the same person.

The point is that any pleasure-seeking activity that becomes an obsession indicates that there are problems with the sacral chakra. A healthy person is able to indulge in nearly any activity without becoming obsessed with it, but if you find yourself with any type of addictive behavior, this is a serious indication that you may have a blocked sacral chakra. It might also indicate that rather than being blocked, you are out of balance. This can result from a blockage in a higher level chakra. As we will see, the heart chakra (as you might guess) is very important when it comes to managing and experiencing healthy interpersonal relationships. If it is blocked, too much energy might gather in your sacral chakra, leading to unhealthy obsessions with sexuality and pleasure.

People with a blocked sacral chakra may indulge in unhealthy or even dangerous sexual relationships, or they may become obsessed with sexuality but react in a way that keeps them from having interpersonal relationships. This is due in part to the association of the sacral chakra with creativity. When there is a hyper-expression of the sacral chakra, if you will, creativity can be expressed in an unhealthy way. In these situations, a person may overindulge in fantasy. This can be done to the point where they achieve satisfaction from fantasy and self-pleasure alone and, therefore, lack a true need for interpersonal relationships of a sexual nature. Unfortunately, the wide availability of pornography online is contributing to this phenomenon, leading many people to withdraw into themselves. If you find that you are overindulgent in fantasy to the point where there is a cost with regard to actual relationships, then you might consider working on your sacral chakra.

For those that do have relationships with other people, they are often unhealthy. This can express itself in the development of co-dependent relationships or dependence on others to help meet your basic needs. This can also be tied to blockages in the root chakra since a person who cannot satisfy their basic needs as an adult can become a drag on others, leading to the formation of co-dependent relationships.

If you have a blocked sacral chakra, one of the ways it can manifest is that you might become the person who is enabling someone else's problems or addictions. If your sacral chakra is not completely in balance, you might try to obtain satisfaction by enabling another person's weaknesses or ill-advised behaviors.

A symptom of this is that you feel low self-esteem. This is something that is more closely tied to the solar plexus chakra, but it is also associated with the sacral chakra, so you are probably going to have to put effort into healing both. In regard to these types of behaviors, you should ask yourself if you are in the position of having to take responsibility for the actions of the person that you are in a relationship with on a continual basis. Does this give you a sense of well-being in doing so, and are you using this to substitute for a healthy way of getting pleasure out of relationships? Also, look to see if you are the person who is always doing more than their share and if you have fears of abandonment. Often, fears of abandonment go back to the root chakra and can be tied to experiences that occurred during childhood. If you find yourself in this spot, spend time healing the root chakra as well as the sacral chakra.

Since the sacral chakra is tied to sexuality, a blocked sacral chakra can lead to feelings of jealousy and fear. Someone who has a blocked sacral chakra will be plagued by inner doubts when

223

it comes to their worth as a sexual being. This can mean that you will also be plagued by feelings of low self-esteem. As a result, even if you are in an active sexual relationship, you will never feel quite adequate or trust your partner. You will experience constant fear that your partner is going to find someone else more attractive, or that they will leave you at any time. This can lead to expressions of jealousy at a rate that creates an unhealthy environment for the relationship.

Depression can also result from a blocked sacral chakra. That is a natural result of an inability to truly experience pleasure, or if you can experience pleasure, you might not be able to manage it in a healthy way. Often, becoming obsessed with pleasure-seeking can lead to destructive behaviors. For example, there is the gambler who ends up losing all the money. The bad situations that can result from addictive behaviors and constant pleasure-seeking can result in depression.

A high threshold for feeling pleasure is also a problematic situation that can result. There are many people around us who have to engage in extreme behaviors in order to feel any kind of pleasure. Some people with a blocked sacral chakra may find themselves engaging in "extreme sports" in order to try and feel any kind of pleasure. Going on a hike does not bring them any satisfaction; they have to rock-climb and do it without equipment, as one simple example. It may manifest in simpler ways, like driving fast and recklessly.

The sacral chakra can be a complicated nut to crack since it can often manifest from seemingly opposite ends of the spectrum when it is out of balance or blocked. That means a higher level of self-awareness and the ability to do some self-examination are going to be necessary in order to deal with a blocked sacral chakra. Of course, the fact that you are reading this book is a good sign that you are already willing to take a look at your life and examine the problems that you are having, so healing the sacral chakra is well within your reach.

Physical Symptoms of a Blocked Sacral Chakra

A blocked sacral chakra is going to manifest itself with the reproductive organs, abdominal area, and the lower back. These symptoms include:

- Impotence: Although the sacral chakra can manifest in obsessive sexual activity when it's out of balance, it can also manifest in ways that inhibit engaging in sexual activity. Sometimes, there are physical causes for these problems, but you should look for other causes first.
- Infertility: Often, infertility problems seem mysterious. Could the sacral chakra play a role? It certainly can, so meditating on the sacral chakra and doing yoga to help open it is one way to get yourself into a healthier state.
- Menstruation problems
- Frequent urinary tract infections
- Kidney problems
- Constipation
- Lower back pain

- Lower abdominal pain
- Appendicitis, but more commonly, the pains that could be associated with appendicitis but never actually manifest as the condition

When it comes to physical symptoms, what you need to be alert when it comes to the sacral chakra are physical symptoms that seem to be manifesting as symptoms alone, as we indicated for appendicitis. If you find yourself feeling pains associated with the disease, but your medical exam comes back clear, or if you are having impotence problems, but your blood flow and testosterone levels are normal, you can suspect a blockage of the sacral chakra.

Meditation for the Sacral Chakra

When working to heal the sacral chakra, surround yourself with the color orange, and drink in its energy. You can fill your meditation room with orange colors, and consider adding orange flowers along with pillows, drapes, and other items. Use orange colored candles to help awaken the sensual energies that are a part of all of us.

Begin as you would with the meditation for the root chakra. Sit quietly in the easy pose position. You can meditate in a quiet room, or use background music if desired. Close your eyes and focus, imagining an inky black background. Begin to see a wheel or a spinning lotus flower with six petals. The wheel/disk or flower should be bright, fluorescent orange in color. See it lighting up the darkness in the same way you could imagine a star lighting up the dark space that surrounds it.

See the light slowly approaching you, and as it gets closer, imagine the spinning proceeding at a faster pace. See it gradually spinning faster, as it enters your body and gradually moves up to your root chakra. Let it sit there for a time, spinning at a constant rate.

Now, see the orange light passing through the root chakra and see it begin to spin faster. Then let the light move further up your body, spinning faster as it rises. See it rise up to the location where you imagine the sacral chakra to be. You can visualize it moving up the lumbar spine, or imagine it coming to a location just below your navel. Keep your eyes closed and breathe deeply throughout the entire session, which should last about 15 minutes. When the disk or flower is in the location of the sacral chakra, see it spinning faster and faster, and it generates more energy.

You can also engage in a color meditation for the sacral chakra. Close your eyes and breathe deeply, focusing on the sensations your body is experiencing. Focus on the energies that you feel in the genital region, and imagine being bathed in warm colors of light ranging from red through orange to deep yellow. See the colors flowing back and forth through the different hues, as you become enveloped in warmth, focusing on the pelvic region. As you inhale, see the color turn bright orange and increase in brightness and intensity. When you exhale, see the color lighten and become yellow. Continue observing your body to heighten your awareness of the sensations your own body experiences. Look for your reproductive organs to hum with life force energy.

Another method of meditation that can be used with the sacral chakra is to meditate while visualizing a spinning ball of light in front of you. Start by imagining the ball of orange light in small form, and then see it grow slightly each time you inhale, and see yourself inhaling some of the orange light coming off the orange ball. Continue this process, letting the orange ball grow with each breath, becoming larger and brighter. Toward the end of the meditation session, you can imagine the orange light filling your entire being.

You can also combine this method of meditation with the VAM chant. Use the VAM chant as you exhale in the previous meditation.

As you become more advanced and you have balanced all of the chakras, you can start to incorporate kundalini chants or mantras in your meditations. However, do this with the utmost care because a kundalini awakening before you are truly spiritually prepared can be negative, even dangerous, or an unpleasant experience.

Five Yoga Poses for the Sacral Chakra

Yoga poses for the sacral chakra will open up the pelvic area and the reproductive/sexual organs. Do not be shy about this; it is perfectly natural and healthy. The key to the sacral chakra is balance, not oppression, guilt, or obsession.

Virasana

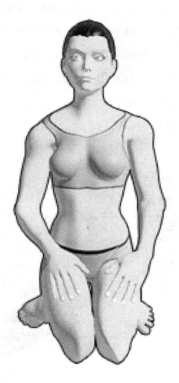

This pose is a kneeling asana that is fairly easy to incorporate into your yoga routine. It will stretch out the knee, thigh, and ankle area. As you become experienced with yoga, you should be flexible enough to move back and forth between the virasana pose and the easy pose with ease. In Sanskrit, virasana means hero pose. It can also be used as a starting position for many other poses.

Description

This is a basic kneeling pose. You can use a pillow or folded blanket. Simply kneel down on the floor on your pillow or blanket. The inner knees should come together, and you bend at the knees. The tops of your feet should be flat on the floor, with your feet pointed backwards, away from you. Sit in the space between your feet – so your feet should be about shoulder width apart. You can turn your thighs inward slightly, and sit up straight. Place your hands, palm down on top of your thights.

Kapotasana

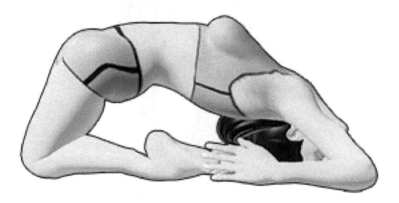

This pose is known as the pigeon pose, and it will expose and open up the pelvic region. You can start for this pose in the virasana pose, and then sit up, and curve your upper body backward until your forehead is on the floor. Use your hands to grab your feet. This will also help to stretch out the lower back region.

Description

Start by going down on your knees, but stand on them with knees about shoulder width apart. Feet should be placed such that the bottom of your feet are facing upwards. Now lead backwards, curving your back around all the way, placing your head face down in between your feet behind you. Then grab each feet with the corresponding hand.

Ardha Hanumanasana

This pose is known as the half splits pose. It will help to open up the legs while stretching out the hamstrings and lower back. It is also known to help increase awareness of the pelvic area, so it is very useful for opening up the sacral chakra.

Description

Stand on your knees, facing forward. Then lift up one foot with your toes. The toes should curl under your foot. Now lean forward with your shoulders so your torso is at a 45 degree angle facing forward with respect to the hip area, and place your arms straight down, giving yourself support with your fingers. Now move the opposite leg straight forward, completely out, and rest on your heel.

Utkata Konasana

Next, we come to the utkata konasana, also known as the Goddess Pose. This is another pose that is helpful for opening up the pelvic region, so it can assist with unblocking the sacral chakra.

Description

Begin this pose from a standing position. Spread the legs outward, each leg at a 45 degree angle, and the feet pointing straight out from each leg. Simultaneously bend downward at the knees while assuming this position, so that you are positions with the knees bent slightly less than 90 degrees. Lift the arms straight up from your sides, stretching them to the ceiling, palms facing inward.

Viparita Virabhadrasana (Reverse Warrior)

The reverse warrior pose is a standing asana that can help you open up the sacral chakra. This is shown below:

This pose is considered to be of recent origin. Nonetheless, it is very useful for opening up the legs and the pelvic region.

As with the root chakra, try and hold each pose for 10-12 slow breaths, and then work your way up to three minutes per pose.

Description

This is a standing pose. Your feet should be facing forward. Now turn to your left – keeping your right foot pointing forward, and stretch out your left leg, pointing away from the shoulder at a 90 degree angle. Bend down with the knee at 90 degrees, while curving your torso about 25 degrees backward toward the right, away from the left knee. The left foot should be pointing outward from the left shoulder about 90 degrees. Lift your left arm upward straight toward the sky, and angle the palm, facing inward, about 15 degrees. Bend the neck slightly so that you are looking straight up at the palm. Repeat for the other direction, switching left and right.

Crystals for the Sacral Chakra

Several crystals can be used when trying to heal the sacral chakra. One of the most popular and effective crystals that you can use when working to heal the sacral chakra is carnelian. This beautiful stone is available at a low cost, and it has a striking, deep orange color. You can use the stone in many ways. For example, you can hold the stones while you are meditating. You can also wear the stone on your body throughout the day when you feel that your sacral chakra is out of balance.

234

Amber is another good stone to use. Amber is an ancient stone that is actually hardened tree sap, and it often contains the remains of ancient organisms like insects that lived long ago. Amber is available in many forms, including necklaces and bracelets.

You can also use a dark, yellowish stone called the tiger's eye for healing the sacral chakra.

Affirmations for the Sacral Chakra

There are many affirmations that can be used to help you heal your sacral chakra. Here are some suggestions; feel free to add your own. Affirmations for the sacral chakra should be said early in the morning and before going to bed, but they can also be said throughout the day. Affirmations are more effective, the more they are repeated.

- I feel at peace and in complete balance.
- My emotions are in harmony.
- I feel love and acceptance, and I let go of jealousy and insecurity.
- I feel comfortable in my own body.
- I feel safe in my relationships.
- Sexuality is my divine right.
- I feel sexual, but I am not overwhelmed by sexuality.
- I feel safe when enjoying sexual activity.
- I am a very creative person.
- My creativity is soaring.
- I release the need to medicate myself.
- I will enjoy pleasure and not try to dull it.

- I feel vibrant and alive.
- I attract healthy and like-minded people.
- I can create, and my creations are valuable.
- I am an imaginative person.
- My imagination is soaring and grows with each passing day.
- My skin is radiant and beautiful.
- My own pleasure is important.
- I will seek to please others but not at the expense of myself.
- I am comfortable.
- I am a being that can nurture others.
- I deserve love and respect from others.
- I feel complete peace within.
- I am passionate about life and enjoy many things.
- I derive great pleasure from a good meal.
- I can enjoy alcohol without being controlled by it.
- I deserve a rich and full life.
-

Sacral Chakra: Concluding Thoughts

The sacral chakra is one of the most important of the lower chakras to open and balance because when it's out of balance, it can have a very significant impact on your life and also on the lives of others. When our sacral chakra is out of balance, it can cause pain in the lives of those who are around us, making us a burden on others. But one of the most difficult aspects when dealing with the sacral chakra is seeing that it can manifest in many different ways when it is a blockage, causing us to either become hyper-pleasure-seeking or shutting ourselves off from pleasure completely. It can also lead to emotional states that can also manifest when there are blockages in other areas. For example, you might have a jealousy problem, and this could result from a blockage in the sacral chakra and/or the heart chakra. When you are not sure about a situation like this, always heal the lower chakra first. Keep this in mind; you cannot have a healthy and fully functioning and unblocked heart chakra if your sacral chakra has a blockage. Use this knowledge to guide your efforts.

Also, we hope that from the discussions we have had so far, you realize that there are several ways to go about opening your chakras. These include meditation, yoga, affirmations, mantras, and simply surrounding yourself with the appropriate color and crystals. You may also note that there can be overlap, and certain psychological symptoms can manifest when there are blockages in different chakras. Insecurity is something that can manifest in the root, sacral, and solar plexus chakra. You can take a deeper look at the problems you are having and look for other signs and symptoms to narrow down the exact chakra that is the source of the blockage in question. It is also possible to do a balancing meditation to work on multiple chakras in one session, as we will be discussing later on in this book.

CHAPTER 4
SOLAR PLEXUS CHAKRA

The solar plexus chakra is another physical or matter chakra. However, we will see that it starts becoming associated with the higher functions of the mind. So it's a less "basic" chakra compared to the other chakras we have examined so far. The solar plexus is represented with 10 lotus petals.

What Is the Solar Plexus Chakra

The solar plexus chakra goes by the name Manipura in Sanskrit. The location of the solar plexus chakra is taken to be the upper stomach or abdominal area, above the navel but below the rib cage and breast bone. The color is yellow to golden yellow. It is symbolized using ten lotus petals with a downward pointing triangle, and you can use an image similar to the one shown above in your meditations or simply imagine a spinning yellow wheel or disk.

The element that is associated with the solar plexus chakra is fire, which indicates this is an energetic chakra. When you come to understand the meaning associated with the solar plexus chakra, this will make sense. The solar plexus chakra is associated with any powerful form of energy, so the sun, heat, or any light energy that is white or yellow in color can be associated with this chakra. It can be helpful to meditate on the solar plexus chakra to the rising sun if this is something that you are able to do.

Although the solar plexus chakra is considered a physical or material chakra, it's more closely associated with mental states and abilities than it is with physical characteristics. It is not as basic as the root and sacral chakras are, and many people view the solar plexus chakra as one that is associated with our professional or career life. The first characteristic that is associated with it is personal self-confidence. In short, everything associated with the solar plexus chakra is going to be something that can be viewed in terms of your ability to lead and get things done. Many historical figures have had open solar plexus chakras; think of Napoleon, Franklin Delano Roosevelt, and JFK as examples of strong leaders who had these characteristics. Many business leaders have open solar plexus chakras, such as Bill Gates, Steve Jobs, Tim Cook, and Jeff Bezos.

But self-confidence is only one aspect of the solar plexus chakra. There are many other meanings associated with the solar plexus chakra that can be tied together with success and leadership. Remember that leadership does not necessarily mean you are the CEO of a company, being a strong leader of self is an important aspect of a strong and open solar plexus chakra.

Taking responsibility is a quality that is seen in those who have an open and balanced solar plexus chakra. This means that you take responsibility for your actions and that you are going to make them right when you have caused problems for others. For example, if you owe a debt, if you have an open and balanced solar plexus chakra, you are going to get the debt paid off promptly. If your solar plexus chakra is blocked, you might have problems making this happen. This last phrase is one that I closely associate with the solar plexus chakra. Think of an open and healthy solar plexus chakra as being something that allows a person to make things happen.

With that in mind, we can come to understand all of the meanings and characteristics that are associated with the solar plexus chakra. Willpower and the ability to make decisions are also associated with a balanced solar plexus chakra. Again, you don't have to be President or CEO of a company; a healthy solar plexus chakra can simply mean that you are able to make decisions for yourself and your own family. At work, you don't have to be a manager or a corporate leader. You just have to be someone that is effective at getting things done, so if you have a balanced solar plexus chakra, you are going to be the employee that your leaders can count on to get things done when you say you are going to get them done. You will approach your work with self-confidence, feeling self-assured that you are able to do any job. You will also have the self-confidence necessary to speak your mind when necessary.

The solar plexus chakra can also tie together with the sacral chakra, both in the personal and the professional realms. On a personal level, someone with a strong solar plexus will be able to ask for and get what they want sexually. In the professional realm, when your solar plexus chakra is healed and fully open, you will be able to tap your creativity from the sacral chakra in order to make things happen in the work environment. Many people who are entrepreneurs have well-developed and open sacral and solar plexus chakras, and this helps to enable them to generate ideas and then turn them into reality. Think about it; many people are creative, but their ideas never come to fruition. Why is that? One reason is that they may have an open sacral chakra, but they have blockages with respect to the solar plexus chakra.

The solar plexus chakra is also associated with a strong personal identity. Your personality will be centered and grounded, and you will be sure of your sense of purpose and who you are. It doesn't matter if this is in the professional realm or in the home, this can be true for stay-at-home parents as well, who are comfortable and confident in their role and the service that they provide. In the career realm, if you have a healthy solar plexus chakra, you will know what you want to do with your life and where you are going. You will be certain about your chosen career and identify with it.

As we said, you don't have to be a CEO or political leader to have an open solar plexus chakra, but an open solar plexus chakra can make this far more likely. This is because an open solar plexus chakra is going to bring about many of the characteristics that are associated with strong leadership. One of these characteristics is going to be decisiveness and clarity of judgment. If you have an open solar plexus chakra, you are going to have a strong sense of self-confidence, as we noted above. This is going to help you make decisions firmly and more quickly because you will have self-confidence in your ability to make decisions and also in your ability to take responsibility for decisions that don't go right. A good leader is someone who is decisive, but they also take responsibility when their decisions turn out for the worse.

Taking responsibility doesn't mean just saying, "I take responsibility." It means setting things right when your decisions have come to create bad situations for other people. Someone with a healthy and open solar plexus chakra will do this naturally, without anyone having to prompt them to do it or tell them that they should. If you find that you are in a situation where you should take responsibility, taking that step of action when you aren't quite sure about it because your solar plexus is partially blocked, can actually serve to help open it up fully.

An open solar plexus chakra will also help you to form strong opinions and beliefs, and you will assert them with confidence. That means you are not going to be forcing them on others, but rather, you will let the beliefs stand or fall on their own while you confidently assert them.

You are also able to set the direction. This can take place on many levels; you can set the direction in your home life. At work, you will be the one who sets the direction and gets others to follow and take action.

Those with an open and healthy solar plexus chakra will find that things seem to go their way all the time. They are able to find the path of least resistance when it comes to accomplishing things. If you have a blocked solar plexus chakra, you may have noticed this characteristic in others, and you might attribute such success to things like "luck." In some people, observing others attain success can even lead to negative emotional states like jealousy.

In summary, then, the solar plexus chakra is associated with:

- You possess self-confidence and the ability to cultivate and access personal power.
- The ability to bring others along with your ideas.
- You have a strong sense of controlling your own outcomes and destiny. And typically, this will be in conjunction with an actual ability to do so.

- You have the ability to transform your creativity from the sacral chakra into the real world.
- You are able to generate ideas and make them happen.
- You are confident in who you are and feel a sense of purpose as far as career or work is concerned.
- You can tap your intellectual powers to the fullest extent possible.
- You are able to lead others.
- You are decisive.
- You take full responsibility for your actions.
- You are assertive but not overbearing or draconian
- You are able to generate expected results.
- You are able to balance personal power with the wants and needs of others.

Mental, Emotional, and Spiritual Signs of Blockage

Since the solar plexus is a more "mental" chakra, you will find that someone with a blocked solar plexus will have many symptoms that impact how their life is "going." If you are someone who can never make things happen the way you want, you might start by taking a look at your solar plexus chakra. This can be on a personal or career level.

A blocked solar plexus chakra can manifest in many ways. Some people with a blocked solar plexus chakra are downright ineffective. If they start businesses, every venture they start either gets nowhere or fails. The person with the blocked solar plexus chakra might be spinning ideas all day long, but they might never take the action steps that are necessary to turn the ideas into reality (this indicates an open sacral chakra, but a blocked solar plexus). At work, a person with a blocked solar plexus chakra might fail to get projects done. Often, a blocked solar plexus chakra can lead you to devote too much energy to details, and this ends up getting in the way of completing important projects.

A person with a blocked solar plexus chakra is the consummate underachiever. In many cases, they will have exceptional innate abilities. They may be highly intelligent and very creative. But because they have a blocked solar plexus, they are never able to get grounded and lack a sense of purpose. They may be completely unsure of what career to pursue, and this can go on for their entire life if the solar plexus is never healed. If they attend college, they will be the smart person who never settles down, and they might continually change from major to major and end up not graduating at all, despite a high level of intelligence.

Apathy is a key characteristic of those with a blocked solar plexus chakra. If you find that you don't have a clear direction for your life, the solar plexus chakra is the place to look for healing. A lack of ambition is often a characteristic closely associated with a blocked solar plexus chakra. This lack of ambition is often covered up by other activities, like excessive consumption of alcohol or smoking marijuana on a daily basis, and then these addictions can be blamed for the circumstances or lack of ambition.

Are you often making plans, but then getting bogged down because your ability to implement and carry out the plans is lacking? This is a definite sign of a blocked solar plexus chakra.

Interestingly, overconfidence is also a sign of a blocked solar plexus chakra. Sometimes, people with a blocked solar plexus chakra will appear confident and assertive, but in truth, they are manipulative, insecure, and abusive. Some people that are in this state will achieve positions of power, and they will use their status to abuse other people. Those who are control freaks also tend to have a blocked solar plexus chakra. A central characteristic of an open solar plexus chakra is that you have supreme self-confidence. Someone who is confident in what they do, what their purpose is, and their ability to lead is not going to be someone who is afraid of letting go of some control. A healthy solar plexus chakra means that you set the direction for others to follow, but you are not going to try and control their every action. A boss or manager in the workplace, or an entrepreneur, who attempts to control every last detail is someone who needs to work on opening their solar plexus chakra.

To summarize, you may have a blocked solar plexus chakra if you experience any of the following:

- You lack self-confidence.
- A feeling that you can't control your own outcomes.

- You don't feel you have the ability to get things done.
- You have lots of ideas, but they never get accomplished.
- You just can't seem to get things to work.
- You feel a lack of purpose when it comes to your role in the home and your career.
- You feel confident but are overwhelmed by a need to be controlling of others.
- You have attained a position of leadership, but you misuse your power and abuse those under your control.
- You feel threatened by the ideas of others.

Some Ways the Solar Plexus Can Be Blocked

Often, the solar plexus chakra becomes blocked during childhood or during adolescence. Anyone who doubted your abilities, intelligence, or your abilities to get things done can close or damage the solar plexus chakra. Parents and other adults who mean well often tell their children that they are "stupid" or not capable of anything. They do this in the hopes that the humiliation will motivate the child to put more effort into their life, but this can often have the opposite effect, causing the solar plexus chakra to become blocked.

This can happen in later years as well. Many women have blocked solar plexus chakras because they have been told at some point that women don't or can't accomplish something. This can happen to men on a less frequent basis. But it doesn't matter who you are; anyone who ever put the thought in your mind that you are not able to get things accomplished or that you lacked abilities could have contributed to a blocked solar plexus chakra.

It can be helpful to pinpoint where in your life these events occurred. But don't dwell on them. It is not going to heal your solar plexus chakra, so you need to move on with your life and leave those past disappointments behind.

Healing the Solar Plexus Chakra Through Meditation

The primary way to begin healing the solar plexus chakra if you suspect you have a blockage is with daily meditation sessions. Remember that the solar plexus chakra is closely tied to the sun due to its foundation that is formed using the element of fire. As such, while it's not required, it can be helpful to meditate for the purpose of healing the solar plexus chakra at sunrise, facing east toward the rising sun, either through an open window or even outdoors. You can feel the power of the sun come upon you through the warmth of your skin during this process. Of course, any time during the day that you can meditate on the sun can be helpful for this purpose, as long as you can do it comfortably.

In your meditation space, fill it with bright yellow colors and light. This alone will have a major impact on your psyche and help to open up the solar plexus chakra. You will find that bright yellow and white colors are going to help you adopt a confident and optimistic attitude, which is an important aspect of an open solar plexus chakra.

You can fill your meditation space with bright yellow and white drapes, open windows, yellow-colored pillows, blankets, and sheets. It can also help to use yellow sheets on your bed during a period where you are working on your solar plexus chakra. You can also wear white and yellow clothing items.

For your meditation, begin using the same techniques used for any meditation session. Your meditation sessions for the solar plexus chakra can last for 15-30 minutes, at least once per day, and up to twice per day. Start in the easy pose, closing your eyes and breathing deeply and rhythmically, with a sense of purpose.

Again, see a black background, with a spinning wheel of light forming in the distance. See it moving closer, spinning at low energy and slow pace. As it enters your body, see it slowly rise up to the point of the root chakra at the base of the spine, spinning gradually faster as it does so.

The spinning wheel or disk should be bright yellow in color. You can visualize the 10-petaled lotus flower shown at the beginning of the chapter if desired. The color yellow is the most important aspect of your visualization.

When it leaves the root chakra, see the disk spinning faster, and have it rise up to the sacral chakra, and stay there for a moment. Then see it leaving the sacral chakra, spinning faster as it rises through your body, approaching the upper abdominal area. Now, see it enter the solar plexus chakra.

Hold it there for several minutes, and see the spinning disk gaining more energy. As it does so, see the disk spinning faster and faster as time passes. Concentrate on the light, and use mantras if desired to enhance your meditation. You can simply use LAM if desired. More advanced readers can use kundalini mantras, but these are not recommended for beginners or those suffering from blocked chakras.

If you like, you can use guided meditations with the solar plexus chakra. I have found this one to be particularly pleasing:

https://youtu.be/84tqM81_XgM

Physical Symptoms of a Block Solar Plexus Chakra

In this section, we will review some of the most common physical symptoms that are seen with a blocked solar plexus chakra. Physical symptoms that are associated with a blocked solar plexus are often closely tied to an inner suppressed anxiety that accompanies either an attempt to project false confidence and control others or the feeling of being out of control that an insecure person may experience.

As a result, when you have a blocked solar plexus chakra, you may experience stomach pains. These can result in a condition called gastritis, and it can also lead to conditions like acid reflux and heartburn. If the condition is allowed to exist for a long time period, you may even develop stomach ulcers. Medical professionals have long known that stress can contribute to the formation of stomach ulcers; this is a virtual certainty if you have a blocked solar plexus chakra.

Blocked solar plexus can also lead to overeating behaviors. These types of behaviors are not only engaged in because of the proximity of the stomach to the solar plexus chakra, but this also occurs an attempt to mask insecurity. One way that many people deal with a lack of self-confidence and a feeling of not being in control of your own destiny is overeating. It brings a temporary sense of comfort, akin to what a drug user may feel from getting "high."

Indigestion is quite common among those with a blocked solar plexus chakra. Depending on the severity of the blockage, the signs of indigestion may be more intense. They can range from excessive gas and burping to irritable bowel disease in long-term cases. You may also experience gall bladder disease, generalized abdominal pains, and even appendicitis. In very serious and long-term cases, diabetes may result, stemming from other behaviors and conditions that can develop as a result of a blocked solar plexus chakra. Of course, overeating to compensate for your insecure feelings can lead to these problems.

Another side effect of this is becoming overweight. This is not to say that all overweight people have a blocked solar plexus chakra; many do not. But you can develop weight problems as a result of a blocked solar plexus chakra, and this can have even more devastating effects because the process of becoming overweight can often sap the self-confidence of many individuals. As a result, you will find it even more difficult to heal from this problem.

Affirmations to Use to Heal the Solar Plexus Chakra

As we have seen with the other chakras, subconscious programming, often done in childhood or adolescence by peers or adults who may even be well-meaning, can lead to blockages. This is a very important issue when it comes to the solar plexus chakra because of its relationship to your self-confidence and ability to carry out plans and actions.

Many of the perceptions we have are the result of the actions of the subconscious mind, and the subconscious mind can even have a large influence over the energy flows through the body and in particular, through the chakras. But one thing about the subconscious mind to remember is that it is basically "dumb," despite the power that it can have over us and our beliefs. You can think of the subconscious mind as a kind of computer program. Just like a computer, it only does what you program it to do. Unfortunately for many of us, bad programming was put in place long ago by others who held influence over us when we were young. So we are not even aware of the programming, that it is there, and how it is influencing our behavior and our thinking patterns.

Becoming aware that this may be impacting your life is a good first step toward healing. This is also why affirmations are often a good way to reverse problems that you are having in your life. Affirmations are nothing more than reprogramming your subconscious mind so that it will carry out new programs that have a positive influence on you and your life.

The programs that make up the operation of or direct the subconscious mind are what end up attracting or repelling certain outcomes, situations, and people in our lives. People are often completely unaware of why they behave the way they do, whether it's failing to hold a job, always getting in debt, or constantly getting involved in destructive romantic relationships. These types of behaviors are all governed by the subconscious, and the programs of the subconscious that make this operate create situations that attract more of the same. Remember that like attracts like.

This more in-depth discussion of these issues in the context of the solar plexus chakra is more important than with the other chakras because the solar plexus helps guide our life as a fully developed and mature adult. This is one reason why it is so closely tied to leadership and career success.

Therefore, if you have a blocked solar plexus chakra, it is my sincere advice that you put a little bit of extra effort into using daily affirmations to help you unblock your solar plexus. Begin with them every single morning, and say them throughout the day as necessary. Repeat each affirmation at least five times. When alone, you can say them aloud if you wish. The more senses that you can involve, the better, as this helps to reprogram the subconscious mind. I have even found that writing affirmations down can help with these thoughts in mind.

The goal of affirmations for the solar plexus chakra is to help you develop a sense of self-worth, self-confidence, and a can-do attitude. With that in mind, here are some suggestions to get started:

- I am confident.
- I am powerful.
- I accomplish what I set out to do.
- My plans are executed effortlessly.
- I am not judgmental of others.
- When I am in a position of leadership, I listen to and take into account the opinions of others.
- I use my power to create good on earth.
- I take action for the benefit of all involved.
- I feel confident and motivated.
- I have a purpose in this life.
- I am in control of the outcomes of my decisions.
- I feel optimistic about the future.
- I have control over my future.
- I will determine my future outcomes.
- I have authentic and compassionate power.
- I feel a sense of inner peace.
- I know who I am in this world.
- I embody confidence.
- I am decisive.
- I take responsibility for the bad decisions that I have made.
- I will not let others control me.

- I find it is easy to get things done.
- I am in control.
- I respect the boundaries of others.
- I release judgment of myself.
- I have high self-esteem, but I also respect others.
- I release the need to be in total control.
- I bring positive energy to any project or undertaking.
- I will complete every project that I start.
- I am careful and pay attention to detail, without obsessing about the little things.

Physical Activity

For healing the solar plexus chakra and keeping it healthy, I also recommend engaging in physical activity to build strength and endurance. The better your physical condition, the more self-confidence you are going to feel. For this purpose, I recommend a combination of weight training and aerobic activity that can include running, biking, hiking, or brisk walking. Your weight training should be general in nature, but you should focus on building core abdominal strength and lower body strength. This will also help you get more connected to the earth and feel strongly "grounded," helping to keep your root chakra open and optimal. The confidence that you gain from engaging in physical exercise will also help the sacral chakra as well. If you engage in regular strength training, this will help you sense your personal power and improve the energy flow through the solar plexus chakra.

Five Yoga Poses for the Solar Plexus Chakra

Now, let's take a look at five yoga poses that are useful for opening the solar plexus chakra.

Balasana (Child Pose)

Begin in a kneeling position. Then bend over forward, bringing your forehead down into contact with the floor. Spread your arms out forward, relaxed. Maintain the position for 10-12 breaths.

Description

Begin in a kneeling position. Then bend over forward, bringing your forehead down into contact with the floor. Spread your arms out forward, relaxed. They should be placed on the floor palms down, with your face in between your arms, forehead resting on the floor. Maintain the position for 10-12 breaths.

Phalakasana (Plank Pose)

This pose will help strengthen the core and abdominal muscles of the body while also strengthening your arms and shoulders. This is an excellent pose for the solar plexus chakra.

Description

Simply assume a push-up position, but stay upright without doing any push-ups. Your body should be angled upward so that your shoulders slope downward, toward your back and ankles. Hold the position for 10-12 breaths.

Virabhadrasana (Warrior III Pose)

This is a more difficult pose. It will not only serve to open the solar plexus charka, but it will help to strengthen the legs and abdominal muscles.

Description

From a standing position, lean forward and stretch your arms out in front of you, bringing your hands together. Then lift your left leg, and stretch it out behind you, angling your body so that you are leaning forward. Hold the pose for 10-12 breaths. Repeat, extending the right leg out instead.

Dhanurasana (Bow Pose)

Description

To assume the bow pose, begin by lying flat on your stomach. Then lift up the backs of your legs, and reach behind to grasp your angles as shown. Hold the position for 10-12 breaths.

Savasana (Corpse Pose)

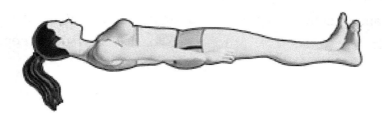

This pose is used for relaxation at the end of your yoga sessions. Some of the poses described in this chapter are going to be difficult for many people, and so this pose will help you come down after your intense session.

Description

This pose merely requires you to lay flat on your back, extend your limbs out and take deep, relaxing breaths. Place your hands, palm up, near the body and spread the legs apart slightly . Feel the muscles of your body enter a relaxed state as you do this.

Crystals to Use for Solar Plexus Chakra Healing

Crystals can also be incorporated into your program to heal the solar plexus chakra. Citrine is the go-to crystal of choice to use with the solar plexus. However, there are several others that can be used. Try lemon quartz, yellow tourmaline, yellow jasper, and tiger's eye. Amber can also be used for the solar plexus chakra.

When you are in a period of working on healing the solar plexus chakra, you can wear these crystals and stones on your body or carry them with you. They can be worn as an amulet, bracelet, or any method that you choose.

They can also be used as part of a meditation session. There are two alternative methods to consider. First, you can try surrounding yourself with the stones as you sit in the meditation position. Alternatively, hold them in your hand, and feel the energy flowing through them as you meditate.

CHAPTER 5

HEART CHARKA

The heart chakra, or Anahata in Sanskrit, is a higher level chakra that is often described as linking together the higher spiritual chakras with the lower physical chakras. It is hard to say whether or not the heart chakra is a spiritual or a physical chakra; in truth, it cannot be pigeonholed or classified in such a manner. The heart chakra serves in both areas of your being and should be viewed as such.

Color and Element of the Heart Chakra

As we move through each of the chakras, from lower to higher position in the body and also from lower to higher functioning, we encounter a higher frequency of vibration. As such, the heart chakra is higher in vibrational frequency than the solar plexus chakra, which is higher in vibrational frequency than the sacral chakra, which is, in turn, higher in vibrational frequency than the root chakra. As we have moved up through the chakras that we have examined in detail so far, we have moved through the colors red, orange, and yellow. The next natural point on the rainbow is green, and you will find that this color resonates well, not only with the energy of the heart chakra but also with its purpose and meaning. We will see this below.

The element of the heart chakra is air. Think of this as free-flowing and encompassing of all that lives, as well as forming the breath of life force. This also expresses the nature of connectivity of all life, as life shares in one breath.

Meaning and Purpose of the Heart Chakra

It won't surprise you that the heart chakra is associated most commonly with the emotion of love. It is also true that this encompasses romantic love as a part of the meaning, but that is not the entire meaning of the heart chakra. If we left it here, the heart chakra would be nothing more than another chakra associated with lower body functions. That is because simply saying it is associated with romantic love is something at the level of a teenager's understanding of love, which is "I" focused or ego-focused love. That is, *I love you, so I have to have you as mine.*

In fact, the heart chakra goes well beyond this, and this is why it is associated more with spiritual chakras. As romantic love develops, think about what happens. It encompasses the needs of the ego, but it also evolves into a higher state of being, where you abandon yourself to form a new union with the other, and the other also becomes as important if not more important than the self.

And there are other types of love and emotions associated with it as well. The heart chakra encompasses all of them. One form of love that might not be immediately obvious is the unconditional love for the self. This is an important aspect of the heart chakra that should not be overlooked. Think about the fact that you cannot truly love another person if you don't love yourself first. This does not mean that we are focused inward and obsessed with our own value. Rather, it means that we accept ourselves and recognize that we have a value that we are able to share with others that are involved in our lives.

The heart chakra is also involved with brotherly and family love. The purest expression of this is the love of your children and parents, as well as the love of your siblings. Parental-type love is also expressed in the love we feel toward our pets. These feelings should come completely naturally to you, but many people actually find this difficult. That is an indication that you have a blocked heart chakra.

The meaning of the heart chakra is also associated with different aspects and components of love. For example, love also involves the emotions and mental states of compassion and empathy. Empathy is actually a highly developed state of being, where you are able to put yourself in the shoes of others so that you can truly appreciate their suffering and hardships. Having compassion for others and being able to forgive are also aspects of the heart chakra.

Acceptance is also an important part of the heart chakra. This starts with acceptance of yourself and your own faults and mistakes that you make along the way of your journey through life. It grows from there to acceptance of others as they are. The more highly developed your heart chakra is, the more you are able to accept others, including others who are not an immediate part of your inner circle in life.

Tolerance is a characteristic that comes out of acceptance. And like some of the other states of being that we have discussed so far in this chapter, tolerance "begins at home," so to speak. That is, you need to be tolerant of yourself before you can be tolerant of others. None of us is perfect, and this is why tolerance is important. That doesn't mean being tolerant to the point where you accept abuse; tolerance is appropriate when the intent of others is good, but they make mistakes along the way. When the intent is bad or evil, tolerance is not appropriate.

The heart chakra is a deeply connected chakra connected to others, to ourselves, and to the universe at large and all of the love energy that it contains. It is also deeply connected to our emotional states; some of them are positive and also negative. When the heart chakra is healed and open, it can easily and freely exchange energy with the environment where you find yourself. You will be able to appreciate all aspects of the beauty around you.

Indeed, the heart chakra is where we begin to find our sense of a higher calling and purpose. The great works of classical music, reflecting our deepest internal emotions, are a reflection of a higher calling outside the self. We also see this in our ability to appreciate the beauty of a sculpture or painting.

A higher calling outside ourselves, including a devotion to a cause, is also something that springs out of the heart chakra. This may express itself in the compassion you feel for the victims of an earthquake or hurricane, even if you have never met them, and they are hundreds of miles away. The heart chakra is able to pick up on their energy and express empathy toward them, often leading many people to take action.

The heart chakra is also important during periods of transition, and this can include the deaths of loved ones. When there is a death in the family, it can be quite traumatic for the soul as we experience the intense emotions of grief. The heart chakra can play an important role during this process, and if your heart chakra is healed and opened, then you are going to be able to deal with and heal from grief in an effective manner. This will help you to maintain the love bonds with those who have passed on, as they have only transitioned into another realm of existence.

An open heart chakra will lead you to have a feeling of being deeply connected. There are no limits as to how far this can go. Some people who are truly spiritually elevated will feel a deep connection to the entire life force of the universe, and they will have a strong connection with family members, friends, and all of those who are around them. For those with the healthiest balance among the chakras and higher spiritual elevation, this connection will spread past the living and to those who have moved on in spirit.

Representation of the Heart Chakra

The representation of the heart chakra includes twelve lotus petals arranged in a circle with two offset triangles that resemble the Star of David. The color is green, which faithfully represents the relatively high-frequency vibrations of the heart chakra that are mid-range in between the root chakra and the crown chakra.

The green color of the heart chakra exhibits a calming effect, which is what the feeling of love will entail when you are coming from a secure point of being.

Mental, Emotional, and Spiritual Symptoms of a Heart Chakra Blockage

It is easy to understand the heart chakra and blockage of the heart chakra. The symptoms of a blockage begin with an inability to establish relationships with other people. For some people, they will drift through life alone and have loose relationships with their immediate family, while being unable to establish lasting relationships on their own. They may be completely isolated and not have children.

Shyness and anxiety relating to social situations are indications that you have a blocked heart chakra. Symptoms of a blocked heart chakra can occur on many levels, some directed inward and some directed outward. You might also express a blocked heart chakra by being too hard on yourself. Try and remember that the heart chakra does not just involve love for others; it also encompasses the love of self, so you should be a lookout for being too difficult on yourself when you make mistakes. This can be hard to recognize because it often takes place on a subconscious level, but you can make yourself aware of it and then be on the lookout for when you are treating yourself in this fashion.

A blocked heart chakra can often reflect past hurts in life. Rejection by a parent or caregiver when you are a small child can have a big impact on the heart chakra throughout the rest of your life. Early or repeated romantic rejections can also have a large impact on the heart chakra. Again, many times, this will manifest itself largely at the subconscious level, so unless you think of things directly, you may not even be aware of the problems that you have that stem from the heart chakra or why there may be a blockage. A long-ago rejection by a romantic interest may be buried deep in your memory, and yet it may be having a very large impact on your mind, soul, and body today.

One way this can show up is in the form of resentment and holding grudges. We all get hurt from time to time because people have conflicting interests, and this can lead to people taking actions that don't take your feelings into account. When this happens, oftentimes, people hold grudges that can last for years. You may have a blockage of the heart chakra that is not directly related to how the grudge is expressed. For example, the blockage may have been caused by troubles in early romantic relationships, but you may hold a grudge against a friend whom you have a platonic relationship with but whom you feel wronged by.

Holding grudges and being resentful are not healthy states of being. The emotional trauma and difficulty that result can manifest in many physical symptoms, some of which we will discuss in the next section.

Another way that a blocked heart chakra can manifest itself is in your ability to freely give to others. Do you feel a tinge of selfishness when you have the opportunity to give to others? This may be the result of the heart chakra being blocked.

Problems with trust can arise when you have a blocked heart chakra as well. Someone who has an open and healthy heart chakra is going to be a person who is able to trust others. They will wait for evidence to emerge that a person is not worthy of trust before they view the person with suspicion. But, if you have a blocked heart chakra, you may find that you view everyone with suspicion from the start. You will be on guard for people hurting you before there would be any indication whatsoever that they will do anything of the kind. You may believe that people are out to get you and take advantage of you and that you should fear close relationships with others.

Physical Symptoms of a Blocked Heart Chakra

The heart itself, as we all know, is directly connected to our relationships with other people, especially when romantic love is involved. Therefore, it should not be a surprise that heart problems can result from a blocked heart chakra, including actual heart disease if the blockage is allowed to manifest over a long time. This can also include ancillary problems like high blood pressure, anxiety, constant worry, chest pains, and sick feelings in the stomach. You may also develop other circulatory symptoms, along with respiratory problems that can include breathing difficulties and asthma.

Meditation for the Heart Chakra

If you need to heal the heart chakra, begin by filling your meditation space with green colors, and seek to wear green colors when possible. You can also use green sheets and bedding materials so that you can envelop yourself in the healing energy that the color green provides.

The first meditation to use for the heart chakra is the basic meditation that uses visualization of a ball of light or lotus flower moving up through the chakras. See a bright green disk of light against the inky blackness of space, coming closer to you, spinning slowly at first. Let the disk of light enter your body and move up through your legs up to the base of the spine. Pause it there, and see the disk begin to spin faster as it gains energy, brightening the darkness with a fluorescent, healing green light. Now, imagine the disk moving slowly up to the sacral chakra. As it does so, begin to see it spinning faster, and then let it leave the sacral chakra and move into the solar plexus. Again, see it spinning faster, letting it pause at each chakra for a few minutes. Finally, let it move up to the heart chakra and see it spinning faster and faster with higher levels of energy, filling your entire chest region with a green light.

In the second meditation, see a ball of green light moving toward you, and see it growing as it gets closer. Eventually, see this large ball of bright green light just before you. Breathe in slowly and deliberately, and begin to take in the green light with each breath. Let the green light fill your chest cavity, and when you breathe out, feel the tension releasing from your heart and chest area.

For our third meditation, use a tool, such as a mobile application, to fill the room with a green light. The key to this meditation is the concept of acceptance and tolerance. You can use affirmations promoting acceptance and tolerance with this meditation, and you can meditate with your eyes open so that you can take in the green light. I recommend doing this meditation at night so that the only light you experience is the green light in the room.

In the fourth meditation, use a green light source, and in this meditation, focus on your breath throughout the meditation. This is a focus meditation where you focus on breath and the green color only. Free your mind completely of any thoughts. Let the experience of the breath and green light direct you where you want to go.

For the final meditation, use a kundalini yoga meditation as taught by Yogi Bhajan. Meditate in a quiet space while repeating this mantra. You can say it aloud or say it with the mind's voice.

"Hate nobody; love everybody. It won't cost you anything. Love never costs anything. Love is the most unselfish act. It gives you so much protection, grace, and radiance. It doesn't give you any smallness or suffering. The attitude of conscious living is to love and give grace to someone worthy of your trust. Do not seek anything from people. Give love instead, and rely on God."

Five Yoga Poses for the Heart Chakra

Yoga poses for the heart chakra can serve to open up and strengthen the chest region. In this section, we will review five of the most popular poses used for healing and opening up the heart chakra. Focus on your breathing while doing these yoga poses.

Marjaryasana (Cat Pose)

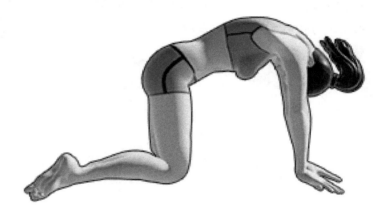

The cat pose will help to stretch out the front of the torso region.

Description

This begins by assuming a tabletop position, with hands and knees on the floor, looking downward. Inhale in this position, and then round the back toward the ceiling as you exhale. When you inhale, return to the normal position and then repeat the process. Perform 10-12 breaths.

Anahatasana (Heart-melting Pose)

This pose is designed to energize the entire body while opening up the heart region. It is simple to do.

Description

Begin in the table pose, with hands and knees on the floor. Then walk the hands out and bring your chest area down onto the floor. Hold the pose for one minute, then repeat as desired.

Bhujangasana (Cobra Pose)

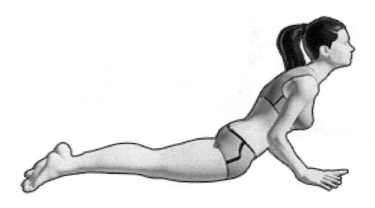

This pose opens up the chest area and also helps to relax the lower back.

Description

Begin this pose laying flat on your stomach, as if to do a pushup, but flat on the floor. Then raise your upper torso up, while leaving the lower body touching the floor, so that you stretch out the chest region. Breathe easily and regularly during the pose, hold for 15 seconds.

Ustrasana

This is a back-bending exercise designed to strongly open up the chest area. Applying care when doing this exercise is necessary. Don't force your neck back any further than it will go; use the repeated practice to make more progress.

Description

In this pose, you will rise up on your knees, and then stretch your arms back to touch the open palms of your hands to your feet, while looking up at the ceiling. Hold the pose for 12-15 seconds.

Setu Banshasana

This is a difficult backbend pose that will open up the chest area.

Description

Lift the upper torso up off the floor. Lay flat on your back, and then raise the knees upward. Stretch out your arms to your sides, palms flat on the floor, positioned near the heels of the feet. Head should be resting flat on the ground. Hold for 12-15 seconds.

Crystals to Use to Heal the Heart Chakra

The primary stone that should be used to help you heal the heart chakra involves those that are green in color. The range of green hues that can be used is quite varied, including jade and emerald. You can also use pink-colored stones with the heart chakra as well, especially if you feel like your blockage is related to a romantic type of love. Rose quartz is the preferred stone for this purpose.

CHAPTER 6

THROAT CHAKRA

In this chapter, we are going to move entirely into the domain of the spiritual chakras. The first of these is the throat chakra, and it might not be entirely clear why the throat chakra is a spiritual chakra. When you think of the throat chakra, you should think about voice and communication. The reason that this is a spiritual chakra is that communication involves conveying information from the inner spiritual world out into the physical world, where it can be received by other beings such as ourselves.

Location, Color, and Element

The throat chakra is located above the heart chakra in the throat region, and it vibrates at a higher frequency than the heart chakra. Therefore, it is more closely associated with the blue color, although turquoise, which is a mixture of blue and green hues, is often associated with the throat chakra.

The symbol of the throat chakra has 16 lotus petals and includes a single upside-down triangle.

The element associated with the throat chakra is sound, which is not surprising, given the central role of sound in human communication.

Throat Chakra Meaning

The throat chakra plays an important role in our lives. The Sanskrit name for the throat chakra is Visshudda, which means purification, a reference to the spiritual nature of this chakra. In addition to the role this chakra plays in simply getting the inner voice to communicate with others in the physical world, you can also think of this chakra as having a role to play in speaking the truth. In particular, think of the throat chakra as being associated with speaking your own truth.

Although the throat chakra is most closely associated with speaking, it is associated with all forms of human communication. This can include nonverbal communication and even the kind of self-talk you engage in with internal communication.

The throat chakra also interacts with and plays a role in the areas that are primarily associated with other chakras. For example, when we discussed the solar plexus chakra, we talked about the ability to make plans and carry them out. Obviously, if you cannot speak your truth and communicate with others, you are not going to be able to carry out your plans. Second, having healthy relationships with others is a part of the heart chakra. But if you

280

can't communicate with the people you have relationships with, then you are not going to be able to have relationships with them, healthy or otherwise.

This indicates that the throat chakra, and the other chakras below it, do not stand on their own completely independently. They interact, and each is required by the other in many circumstances.

The throat chakra is also involved in spiritual communication. Having a healthy throat chakra will help you pray more effectively and even help you communicate with past loved ones.

Finally, the throat chakra is involved in your sense of purpose. This includes your chosen occupation or career, role in family life, and role in the world, generally.

Emotional, Mental, and Spiritual Symptoms of a Blocked Throat Chakra

When you have a blocked throat chakra, you are going to have problems communicating. This can often manifest in an inability to speak out when it is necessary or desirable to speak your truth. You might have difficulty expressing your feelings to someone you are romantically involved with. Or maybe, you are being treated unfairly at work, and you will have a problem communicating this to your superiors. In general, you might have an inability to communicate your ideas and thoughts to others. This can be at work or in the home environment.

In many cases, a blocked throat chakra will make you nervous about speaking up. This can happen in any situation. If you feel that you have problems communicating your ideas, that speaking them out makes you nervous, or that you can't communicate your own personal needs, then you may be suffering from a blocked throat chakra.

Social anxiety and shyness is a clue that you have a blocked throat chakra. You may also have a lot of creative thoughts, but you feel as though you can't tell anyone about them, and you worry that they are perceived as stupid.

If your actions and words are inconsistent, this is an important indicator of blocked throat chakra. This can create a self-feedback loop as well, leading to an increased blockage. The reason is that other people are going to be observing the fact that your words and actions are inconsistent. That will lead them to trust you even less than they do now, and then in the future, your words will be held in even less regard. You will either recognize this explicitly or sense it, leading to heightened social anxiety, less willingness and ability to speak on your part, and more problems communicating your ideas in the future.

People with a blocked throat chakra will develop a cynical attitude since they are not able to communicate effectively. This can also cause them to become stubborn and withdrawn.

Physical Signs of a Blocked Throat Chakra

It won't be surprising to note that a blocked throat chakra can result in laryngitis. So at least on a temporary basis, you will lose

282

the ability to communicate vocally in its entirety. Be especially aware of this if this happens on a persistent basis. Repeated sore throats can also be a symptom of a blocked throat chakra, especially if no medical cause is found. The real problem with the sore throat may be that it's arising in order to give you an excuse not to communicate verbally with others. Less dramatic physical issues that can come about because of your discomfort with speaking to others include hoarseness, neck pain, and dental problems. Some people will develop ulcers in their mouths and have headaches.

Meditation for the Throat Chakra

When meditating on the throat chakra, use the color blue. You can use whatever shade you like, including darker blue hues, but softer blue tones are often associated with the healing of the throat chakra. Fill your meditation space with blue colors, and you can also do this with your living space generally. Use blue drapes and other items throughout the home. The blue color will help to induce a calming effect that will make your meditations more effective.

You can use any of the standard methods that were described in previous chapters for meditation. When light is used, soft blue light is preferred for the throat chakra. When meditating for the throat chakra, although your eyes should be closed, imagine focusing them on the tip of the nose.

For method one, use the Humee Hum mantra to chant while meditating.

While meditating on the throat chakra, due to its role in verbal communication, it can be very helpful to incorporate mantras and vocalizations into your meditation. If necessary, make sure you are alone while doing this as you may have issues with social anxiety while speaking out, and you may fear mockery by others. The key to healing the throat chakra is to avoid trying to overcome too much at once.

Five Yoga Poses for the Throat Chakra

The following yoga poses can help open up the throat chakra.

Sukhasana

You can simply use the easy pose to help you with the throat chakra. Consider holding the pose with your hands together in prayer, about 3-5 inches in front of your chest area.

Description

Sit on the floor, with legs crossed in front of you. Hold your back straight, and form the prayer position with your hands, positioned at the chest area, about 4 inches in front of the center of your chest.

Matsyasana

This is the reclining backbend asana, which will arch your back and stretch out and curve the throat area. Lean backward from the easy pose position to do the Matsyasana.

Description

Sit in the easy pose position, with legs crossed in front of you, but with bottoms of your feet turned upwards. Place your hands palms down at your sides, with wrists aligned with your hip area and fingers pointing straight forward. Then lean backwards as far as you can comfortably go. Work to turn the head back so that the crown of your head is resiting on the floor.

Alternatively, you can do the pose with the legs stretched outward.

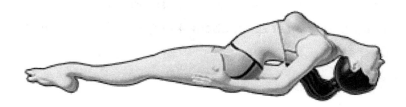

Salamba Sarvangasana

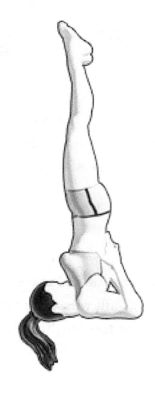

This pose is not recommended for beginners. It will bend the neck quite severely. This pose is known as an inversion pose, but it will help strengthen the throat chakra.

Description

Start laying flat on the floor, with feet together. Then raise your feet straight up to the ceiling, positioning them so your toes are pointed straight up at the ceiling. Support the back with your hands, turned inward to the back. Keep your shoulders, neck, and head resting flat on the floor.

Purvottanasana

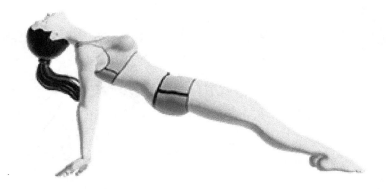

Unlike the last pose, this one is designed to open up the throat and chest area, helping to open the throat and heart chakras.

Description

Lay flat on the floor, and position the hands at the shoulder area, with fingers pointing in the direction away from your body. Push your body up, leaving feet pointing straight out away from you on the floor. This can be visualized as doing a kind of pushup but with the front of your body facing upwards.

Cat-Cow With Lion's Breath

For this pose, get on all fours, on your hands and knees. This is called the cow pose. Inhale through the nose. Then you will exhale in the method of a cat roar, with the intention of toning the back of the throat and exhaling out strongly. As you exhale, stick your tongue out, down toward your chin in cat fashion. This will help strengthen the muscles used in vocal communication, including the throat and the tongue. Your hands can face forward or backward.

Description

Sit on your knees, with legs spread at a 45 degree angle. Support yourself with palms down on the floor, but with your hands turned backwards, straight inward. Lean forward about 40 degrees, and open your mouth, sticking the tongue out to mimic a cat.

Crystals for Healing the Throat Chakra

There are three main crystals that are preferred for healing the throat chakra. Turquoise is one of the best stones to use as a part of your healing efforts. Since turquoise combines green and blue hues into a single bluish stone, it can help to involve your heart chakra in the healing process. Why is this important? Because it will help you speak your truth and get your actions more consistent with your words. You can also use lapis lazuli, which is a deep blue stone that is quite striking in appearance. Another stone that is useful for the healing of the throat chakra is sapphire.

CHAPTER 7
THIRD EYE (AJNA)

The third eye is a truly spiritual chakra. It is through the third eye that we obtain our abilities to be intuitive. Those who have opened the third eye to the fullest extent possible may have a "third eye awakening" that enables them to sense, use, and exploit psychic powers.

While the throat chakra is a spiritual chakra, the difference between it and the third eye is that the throat chakra is involved in the communication of information from within to others who are in the physical realm. The third eye, on the other hand, is connected to higher dimensions, so to speak. Through the third eye, you can communicate with the universal consciousness and spirit beings.

This will also help you to develop and become in closer contact with your higher self.

Location, Color, and Element

The third eye is located in the center of the brow, just above the eyes. It is also closely associated with a small organ in the brain called the pineal gland. The pineal gland is essential for a fully functioning third eye, and many experts recommend decalcifying the pineal gland. Calcification of the pineal gland through excess calcium in the diet and other factors like fluoride in the drinking water can have a negative impact on the functioning of the third eye. The details of pineal gland calcification are beyond the scope of this book due to space limitations, but you can learn about this elsewhere, and there are many free references on the web about this topic.

The color associated with the third eye chakra is indigo. The third eye is vibrating at a very high frequency with respect to the lower chakras, and this is largely because of its primarily spiritual nature. Indigo is a near purple color and, therefore, is close to the highest possible frequencies of visible light in the rainbow.

Appropriately, the element of the third eye is light. This reflects the spiritual nature of this chakra, as light cannot be contained, and it travels at the highest possible velocities. Also, note that light is able to assume many different forms in the different colors that we perceive.

Meaning of the Third Eye

The third eye chakra is closely associated with the mind and with the so-called sixth sense, which is psychic intuition. The third eye is also considered to occupy a "supervisory" role with respect to the lower chakras. So, if you have an out of balance third eye, this can lead to problems down the line as well.

Until now, all of the chakras that we have examined to one extent or another are focused on ego. Granted, the higher up you go among the chakras, the higher the functioning. However, the ego is still involved even with the throat chakra. The third eye is where we encounter the notion of letting go of the ego. A large part of your spiritual awakening is going to involve letting go of ego, and this will be accomplished by opening up the third eye.

The third eye has practical, as well as spiritual aspects. Many creative people are able to visualize very well. They can do this in the "mind's eye," and this can help them to take their creativity to another level. This type of visualization is actually derived from the third eye chakra. If you think of someone who is a great visionary and their ideas seem to "come out of nowhere," think about how the third eye may be playing a role in generating ideas and pushing them forward. Many of the world's greatest scientists such as Einstein and Newton must have had third eye awakenings, even if they would not refer to their insights in such a fashion.

The third eye allows you to connect with the universe at large, including the universal consciousness and the spiritual realm. Often, if you have an open third eye, you will find that information is coming to you as if it is suddenly known, or it is presented to you in dreams. Sometimes this information can even be of a practical nature. Many people with well-developed third eyes will report that they suddenly see or receive the solution to a difficult problem. The types of problems solved in this manner can be of any nature. They can include a problem in a relationship, but in many cases, it might be a practical problem like fixing something in the house, or a scientist will suddenly "know" the solution to a difficult problem in mathematics.

A common aspect of an open third eye is that you will experience lucid dreaming. Again, this can take many forms. People who experience lucid dreaming will often find that they dream very realistic dreams about events that have not happened yet. In some cases, the events will happen exactly as they play out in the dream. In other cases, the dream only represents possibilities that the future may assume but is not guaranteed to do so.

Many people experience lucid dreaming about past life experiences. Whether or not you believe in reincarnation, these types of dreams do occur, and they happen often to millions of people. It is hard to say if they actually represent past lives or if they represent psychic insights into future events that are revealed in the context of past histories.

The main feature of the third eye is intuition. We all experience intuition in one degree or another, you might "know" when someone is about to call you on the phone, for example. Some people may "know" there is about to be a plane crash. These are basic levels of intuition that we all experience.

By working to unblock your third eye, you can enhance intuitive abilities like these and increase their occurrence.

Emotional and Spiritual Symptoms of Blockage

One symptom of a blocked third eye is a skeptical attitude. When your third eye is completely blocked, you will experience no intuitive abilities at all, so it will be easy to dismiss the psychic realm. People with a blocked third eye often have other blockages as well, and this can lead them to have a resentful attitude that is expressed as skepticism.

On the other hand, some people will have dysfunctional expressions of the third eye when they have a blockage. This can be mild, in which case they will experience chronic depression and anxiety. It can also take on a more intense form where they become overwhelmed by paranoid thoughts and even delusions in more serious cases.

The best thing to do is to catch a blockage in the early stages. If you are finding yourself feeling depressed (but not clinically) and having paranoid thoughts, the time is now to start working on the third eye chakra.

Physical Symptoms of Blockage

Vision problems are often related to a third eye blockage. If you find that you often see lights that aren't really there, this can be a symptom. This is often accompanied by migraine headaches. In severe cases, seizures can result. You may also experience neck aches in the back of the neck or localized headaches in the back of the head (where the vision centers of the brain are reported to be located).

Meditation for the Third Eye

In this section, we will consider five third eye meditation techniques. As with other chakras, you will want to surround yourself with the color that is associated with the chakra, but with the third eye, you do have a little bit of flexibility. You can use dark blue, purple, violet, or indigo colors.

The first meditation technique that I will propose is focusing on the brow. You can literally feel the opening of the third eye, with the energy in the central portion of the brow. Sit in the easy pose position, and close your eyes. You can include some calming background music with this if you prefer. Draw your attention to the location of the third eye at the center of the brow, just above the level of the physical eyes. Now, become aware of the energy that is flowing through the third eye. Focus on this location for the entire meditation session, breathing in and out slowly and regularly. Do not think of anything else, and let your mind be free to whatever comes to it while focusing on the third eye. Be very conscious of the sensations that you feel and look for a third eye-opening. You may feel tingling sensations and energy flowing through the third eye.

For the second method of meditation, we will use the standard method applied with the other chakras. This time, visualize a bluish/purplish light in the form of a disk against the darkness of space, slowly approaching your body. As it closes in on your

296

body, see it spinning slowly, and then entering your body and moving upward toward the root chakra. See it move up to the root chakra and remain there for at least two minutes, breathing deeply in a relaxed fashion. Now, see the disk begin to gain energy, spinning faster as it leaves the root chakra and reaches the sacral chakra. Now, hold it there again for two minutes. Repeat this process as it passes through all of the chakras, spinning faster as it rises through your body. Finally, end the meditation after it has reached the third eye. Concentrate on any sensations you feel in the third eye during the meditation.

For the third meditation technique, picture a ball of purple light in front of you. As you breathe in, imagine the light going through your third eye into the pineal gland. Then breathe out, and see the energy emerge from your pineal gland and out to the ball of light. Keep this going for about 15 minutes.

The fourth method of meditation you can use with the third eye is guided meditation. Use a video you like from YouTube for this purpose. Try and focus on the imagery and listen to the sounds while freeing your mind of any thoughts during this process. The absence of thought will be key to opening the third eye.

Finally, we consider the focus method. This is similar to guided meditation and also to trataka (see below). In this method, however, I will propose you use a single purple light provided by a meditation app on your phone if possible. The goal, in this case, is to focus on the light for a timed meditation of ten minutes, completely emptying your mind of all thought. Let the experience of the color purple fill your entire being without letting a though intrude.

The absence of thought will help you to open your third eye because the third eye is psychic in nature. That is, the logical mind gets in the way of our ability to receive psychic imagery and messages. By calming the logical mind, we can help to open the third eye and give the spiritual plane of existence more room that can be used for communication.

Five Yoga Poses for Third Eye Healing

In this section, we will consider yoga poses that can help you open your third eye chakra.

Trataka

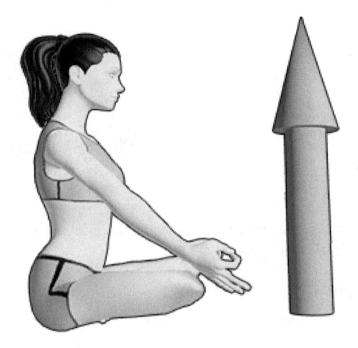

This is not so much a yoga pose, as it is a clearing of the mind. The goal is to focus on a single object and free the mind of all thoughts, coming into complete focus on the chosen object. The common example used is the flame of a candle.

Description

Spend 10 minutes focusing on the tip of the candleflame in the darkness. This is useful because of the role of the third eye in the spiritual and psychic realms.

Balasana (Child Pose)

The child pose was discussed earlier. It can also be used to help heal the third eye chakra.

Description

Assume the tabletop formation, on your hands and knees. Lower your knees to the floor, with feet turned upward, turning your knees at a slightly wide angle larger than the hips. Lower your hips to touch the heels of your feet, and walk your hands forward until they are stretched out as far as they can go. Place palms flat on the floor and lower your head in between the hands, touching your forehead to the floor.

Prasarita Padottanasana

This pose will open up the root and sacral chakras as well. Form an energy conduit between the earth through the feet, then through the body, and back to the earth through the third eye. By positioning the forehead on the floor in this pose, you will open up the throat area strongly.

Description

This pose begins from a standing position. Spread your legs apart, wider than shoulder width. Then bend over as far as you can go. The goal is to touch the crown of your head to the floor. This will stretch out the back in addition to opening the third eye.

Nadi Shodhana Pranayama (Alternating Breath)

This is also known as channel cleaning breath.

Description

Sit in easy pose position. The goal of this exercise is to breathe through alternate nostrils. Begin by plugging the left nostril, and breathe deeply through the right nostril. Then plug the right nostril while freeing the left nostril, and breathe deeply through the left nostril. This exercise is believed to purify the subtle energy channels in the body.

Ardha Uttanasana

This exercise is also called half-forward bend. It is a relatively straightforward pose.

Description

Start from a standing position with legs about shoulder length apart, then bend over forward and touch the floor with the tips of your fingers. Hold the position for 10-12 breaths.

Affirmations for the Third Eye

In this section, we will list some affirmations you can use to help open and strengthen your third eye chakra.

- I have intuitive abilities.
- I am more than just a material, physical being.
- I can connect with the entire universe.
- I have psychic abilities.
- I am able to experience lucid dreaming and can interpret the messages in my dreams.
- I am open to a world that lies beyond the five senses.
- I am willing to communicate with the Universe.
- I will accept any information that is given to me.
- I trust my intuition.
- I trust any guidance I receive from the psychic gifts I have.
- I feel safe when receiving the guidance of a higher power.

Crystals for Third Eye

The main crystal that is used for the third eye is purple amethyst. It often has white and other colors in it, but it is very spiritual in its frequency and well-suited for the third eye.

CHAPTER 8
CROWN CHAKRA (SAHASWARA)

Finally, we reach the crown chakra, which is the highest of all the chakras. It is here where you meet your Higher Self and experience the spiritual nature of the universe. You can also connect to the Universal Consciousness and Spirit Guides by opening the crown chakra. It won't surprise you to learn that most people have a blocked crown chakra.

The Sanskrit name of the crown chakra is Sahasrara, which means a thousand petals.

Location, Color, and Element

The crown chakra is located on the top of the head, but many experts take the crown chakra to actually be slightly above the top of the head. This is due to the spiritual nature of the crown chakra. The crown chakra should be thought of as being primarily spirit. It is also closely associated with thought.

The crown chakra is associated with the colors purple, white, and gold. These are the royal colors, and they also represent high energy in the form of purple and purity in the form of white.

The element of the crown chakra is thought itself. Others associate all five of the basic elements with the crown chakra. These are not elements in the scientific sense but, rather, in the spiritual sense. The five elements of the crown chakra are ether, air, fire, water, and earth. By incorporating all of these five elements, the crown chakra serves a unifying purpose, as well as a spiritual purpose. This is important because the crown chakra represents the focal point of unity that makes you a complete being, with roots in the physical, emotional, mental, and spiritual worlds.

Meaning of the Crown Chakra

The meaning of the crown chakra is highly developed spirituality. Through the crown charka, you can get in contact with your higher self and increase your spiritual awareness. Opening the crown chakra is necessary before being able to move on to any higher spiritual development, such as a kundalini awakening. If you seek higher spiritual development, a fully developed and open crown chakra is a definite pre-requisite to this.

The crown chakra is highly associated with self-consciousness and self-awareness. However, it is not limited to our own being.

306

It is through the crown chakra that we are able to establish a connection between ourselves and the illusion of our individual being and the rest of the universe. The connection that can be established through the crown chakra is said to be formless and timeless.

The crown chakra is also the seat of wisdom and discernment. We can develop many abilities through the other chakras, but applying them without true wisdom is foolhardy. That is why meditating on the crown chakra is something that needs to be a part of your spiritual journey.

The crown chakra also enables us to join together in oneness with the spiritual side of the universe. You will find that you are able to enter into communion with the Higher States of Consciousness and the Creator when you have a fully open crown chakra. Some people also report that they are able to meet with and communicate with Spirit Guides, and it is even possible to meet with and communicate with deceased loved ones who have moved on to an existence in the spiritual realm.

These types of communications can lead to a sense of incredible contentment and feelings of peacefulness and joy. It will also help you to feel real and present in the now.

Emotional and Spiritual Symptoms of Blockage

As we mentioned in the opening of this chapter, unfortunately, most people are actually suffering from a blockage of the crown chakra. Or, they have an open crown chakra, but it is not balanced. Let's consider the first case.

When the crown chakra is blocked, this can lead to a feeling that your life has no purpose. It can also manifest in feelings of being disconnected from the spiritual side of life. A belief in militant atheism can arise when you have a blocked crown chakra since the truth is you are not able to access the spiritual energies that are all around us.

Practical consequences can also result. When people have a lack of spirituality, this can lead to many forms of apathy. You may feel disconnected and lack direction in your life. This is important to think about because similar symptoms can result from blockages of other chakras. One clue that the crown chakra is the root cause of your problems is that you may feel socially isolated, even if you have a lot of close friends and family. Desperate feelings of loneliness are common among those who have a blocked crown chakra.

Physical Symptoms of Blockage

Neurological disorders and headaches are common among those with the blocked crown chakra. This can include isolated nerve pain, but migraine headaches are common. If problems related to a blocked crown chakra are left alone, this can lead to the development of more serious problems related to the nervous system, including dementia and tumors. Less serious problems can also arise, such as insomnia and difficulty concentrating. Some people may develop Parkinson's or Alzheimer's disease.

Meditation for the Crown Chakra

In this section, we will consider five different meditation methods for the crown chakra. For the first method, we will consider a basic opening meditation for the crown chakra. This meditation can last about 15-30 minutes.

Begin in the easy pose, and close your eyes, visualizing a ball of white and purple light, with touches of gold. See it spinning as it approaches you from deep space and enters the body. Now, visualize this ball of light rising up through your body to the root chakra. Let it pause there, to heal the root chakra, and help you seek balance. Then see the ball of light gain energy and spin slightly faster as it rises up to pause at the sacral chakra. Repeat the process until the ball of light, now spinning fast, rises up to the crown chakra, and then envision a beam of white light emanating from the top of the head.

In the second meditation, we will focus on the crown chakra in isolation. For this meditation, you can sit in the easy pose again, resting your hands on your knees with palms upward. Now, visualize a thousand-petaled lotus just over the top of your head. See this lotus in vibrant colors of purple, white, and gold. As it spins, visualize small specks of golden energy coming off the spinning disk.

You can use a mantra with this meditation, "I am bathed in divine light, which protects me and opens me to the universe." As you say the mantra, feel the warm light from the energy lotus over the top of your head. Now, see the spinning lotus entering your body and flowing through it, moving downward through each of the seven major chakras. Focus all of your senses on the light. You can see its bright brilliance and feel its warmth. Imagine touching the light and feeling the heat, and try imagining the smell of a beautiful lotus flower.

As the light flows through your body, feel it awaken every single cell to the universal consciousness and the connection to your Higher Self. Let the energy surge as it passes through your lower chakras and, finally, as it exits the body. Breathe deeply as darkness and peace returns, and open your eyes.

In the third meditation, you can use the focusing technique discussed in the last chapter. I like to use three candles, one gold, one purple, and one white, placed close together at a distance that is far enough so I can focus on the three flames simultaneously. Light the three candles, and empty your mind of all thoughts, focusing totally on the flames. Let whatever comes into your mind come into your mind, and try to focus intently on the flames for 15 minutes.

Next, consider merging meditation. In this meditation, begin at the root chakra, focusing on the element earth. Then visualize the earth dissolving into water, now focusing on the sacral chakra. After concentrating on this for a few minutes, let the fire consume the water for the solar plexus chakra. Then see the fire extinguished by air, as it will be by the heart chakra. Then let the air become ether, to represent the throat chakra. Now, transmute the air into the purple light of the third eye. Finally, see the light dissolve into the bright white light of the Universal Consciousness. This meditation will help you experience unity and balance all of the chakras in a single meditation.

Finally, try this meditation, focusing on the creative sound OM. Let your mind hear it, rather than consciously saying it. In this meditation, start by seeing a beam of light that is purple in color, emanating from the crown of your head, and have it meet a beam of purple light coming down from the heavens. Then visualize the beam passing down through your body, going through each of the seven chakras. First, it will enter your body through the crown chakra and then pass through the third eye at the location of the pineal gland.

Then see it passing through the throat chakra. Visualize the beam moving slowly and methodically as it passes through each of the seven major chakras. Now, let it go through the chest area and through the heart chakra. Finally, it will go down through the solar plexus, sacral chakra, and then down through the root chakra. Then let it pass through to the earth while still seeing the top of the beam connected to the heavens. So, at this point, you will be visualizing the entire beam of light passing through the body and connecting the heavens and earth through your seven major chakras.
Use about 15-30 minutes for this meditation.

Five Yoga Poses for Crown Chakra Healing

In this section, we will cover five yoga poses that are helpful for crown chakra healing.

Ardha Padmasana or Half-Lotus Pose

This is a similar pose we discussed in the previous chapter. It will actually serve to open many energy centers, and provide stretching for the backs of the legs, lower back, arms, and shoulders.

Description

Stand with feet shoulder length apart. Bend over, keeping your legs straight, and touch the floor with your fingers. Palms should be facing backward toward the body. Now arch your head up slightly, so that the crown is pointing upward.

Vriksasana or Tree Pose

The tree pose can help you direct energy to the crown chakra, which will help it to open and heal. The hands are held above the head in prayer position while you stand on one leg, using one leg in a padmasama position. You may wish to alternate legs used for each position, and so repeat the pose with left leg up and then with right leg up.

Description

Stand with feet shoulder length apart. Raise the arms up, and form the prayer position with hands above the head, arms stretched upward as high as they will go. Lift one leg and place the foot flat against the opposite thigh.

Salamba Sirsasana or Supported Headstand

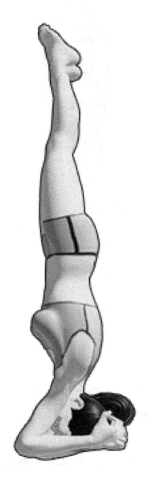

This is a more advanced pose that will send energy through the crown chakra. Basically, this is a headstand position. Work your way up to doing it for short periods of time until you get used to the position.

Description

Form a headstand position, with the top of the head against the floor, flat. Stretch the legs out straight, keeping the feet together, pointed toward the ceiling at a 45 degree angle. The arms should be positioned so that you can clasp your hands together at the back of the head.

Paschimottanasana

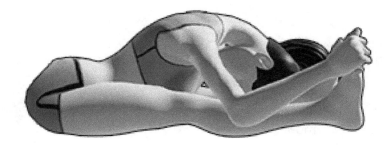

This pose is relatively easy to do. This is often used to open the crown charka, but it will also provide the benefit of stretching out the back area.

Description

This is a seated pose, with your legs stretched out in front of you. Then lean over forward with your face going to the floor in between your legs, while you grab your feet out in front of you.

Rabbit Pose (Sasangasana)

The final pose we consider for the crown chakra is called the rabbit pose. This pose not only serves to physically open the chakras, it will also serve to put one in a prayerful and contemplative mood.

Description

This pose is done from a kneeling position, beginning from the child pose. Lean forward with face to the floor while you grab your feet.

Affirmations for the Crown Chakra

Below are some affirmations that you can use for the healing of the crown chakra:

- I am at peace.
- I feel at home in this Universe.

- I feel connected with this Universe.
- I am protected by the Divine Light.
- I am connected to my Spirit Guides.
- I am grateful for my Life and this Universe.
- I experience Oneness with the Universe.
- I feel Pure Love from the Universe.

Crystals for Crown Chakra

Purple amethyst is an excellent crystal to use for the crown chakra. Any white or glassy crystal is also good. White quartz works well, as well as clear quartz. You can even use gold for the crown chakra.

CONCLUSION

Thank you for making it to the end of *Chakra Healing*. Let us hope it was informative and able to provide you with all of the tools you need to achieve your goals, whatever they may be.

This book gives you an introduction to the seven major chakras. You can begin to use the knowledge conveyed in this book to work on your own healing and start leading a life of balance and contentment. However, this book is only the beginning of a spiritual journey. It is my hope that you will continue your study of the seven chakras, energy healing, meditation, yoga, and crystals. I have written many books in a series, and it is my hope that if you found this book useful, you will continue your study by reading the rest of the books.

In addition, I encourage readers to seek out a good yoga class to help them incorporate yoga into their lifestyle. You can also incorporate daily meditations into your routine to keep your chakras healed and in balance. You can also seek out many tools online for guided meditations whenever you need additional assistance with your healing.

May you find peace, joy, and harmony in your life.

CPSIA information can be obtained
at www.ICGtesting.com
Printed in the USA
LVHW050939080121
675636LV00001B/85

9 781914 032295